THE DOUBLE VIEW

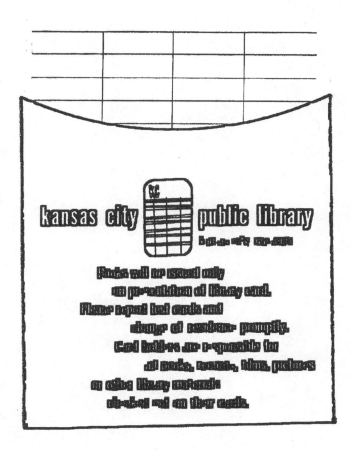

THE
DOUBLE
VIEW

DESIGNED BY WILLIAM R. MEINHARDT
PRINTED IN THE UNITED STATES OF AMERICA
BY THE HADDON CRAFTSMEN, SCRANTON, PENNA.

for
Sally and Iris and Marie

THE
DOUBLE
VIEW

1

HE WATCHED THE white-uniformed
young nurse coming down the walk toward him. Her
head was bowed as if in prayer. Suddenly she looked
up, stared directly into his eyes, and then they were
smiling at each other. Two human beings sharing,
out of embarrassment (for what, pray God, was *anybody* doing there!), a surprise of sunshine, a moment
of untrammeled circumstantial rapport.

In that split smiling second someone in the asylum
building howled, "Catch him! Catch him!"

Smiles stunned, they both jerked their heads toward
the building.

"There he *goes!*" the voice screamed again.

The screen on a third-floor window smashed away,
the green-clad body of a patient, as though thrown,
hurtled headfirst into space after the screen and,
writhing in agony, in sudden mid air, fell the three

11

floors and thudded back first to the concrete sidewalk.

"Jackson! Jackson!" the young nurse shouted, and rushed to the moaning body.

As Rand, in terrified shock, glared, almost in anger, at the body, glistening Negro attendants and starch-white nurses were dashing out of the building and the windows were jammed with the craning heads of green-jacketed male inmates. Visitors like himself crowded around on the sidewalk, and a shabbily dressed old lady began to whimper softly, like a small frightened animal caught in a trap. Rand looked up again at the gaping window on the third floor and Carter's thin castigated face suddenly appeared there, framed.

Surprise, then fury, surfed over Rand. "Did you do it?" he shouted accusingly up at Carter. "Did you?"

Carter frowned down at him, then laughed. "Of course not, you crazy bastard. What do you think I am—a murderer? That poor idiot has tried to knock himself off three times since he's been here."

Rand was very much relieved. His thinking Carter had something to do with this horrible incident was stupid and, he felt, really quite unforgivable. The crowd was still around the moaning would-be suicide, and two doctors were dutifully attending him before rolling him onto the waiting stretcher. Rand yanked his mind away from the misery there and walked into the huge red-brick building to sign Carter out for the afternoon. He had to push through a cluster of gawking, awed visitors to get inside the door.

"He bleeds," someone whispered.

"What made you think I pushed him?" Carter asked Rand. They were sitting on the grass near the serene iron fence that enclosed all the hospital grounds.

"I'm not entirely sure," Rand replied. "Partly, perhaps, because I think you might do such a thing, and partly because in that moment I was really identifying myself with you, so I was upset because it seemed that I had done it."

"Is that why you come to see me? Because you think that I am you—or some alternate of you?"

Rand laughed. "Right! You're my double. You're doing my time for me, you had my breakdown."

Carter shook his head and began plucking at helpless blades of grass between his crossed legs. Rand gazed around the asylum landscape. On a cleanly contoured knoll behind them a green patient was lying with his head in the lap of a girl, as though asleep, his head turned into her soft belly, while she stroked his hair. Down by the iron fence—each bar was a spear—two more green figures stood talking.

Rand could not hear them; holding on to the iron spears, they seemed like figures frozen in a lunatic ballet, arms this way, legs that way. And here and there, dotting the distant lawn and knolls, beside the inevitable lonely trees, moved slow-motion figures, some in green, some in street black, holding hands, or heads bowed, or munching tidbits eagerly brought in from outside.

I wonder if he's still crazy, Rand thought, looking now at Carter. You never know, they're so tricky.

"I went up before the magicians yesterday," Carter remarked.

"And what happened?"

"They decided not to plug me in anymore."

"Plug you in?"

"Yes—AC, DC. Shock."

"Oh."

"You sound disappointed."

"Don't be absurd." Oh, oh, here he goes.

"You wouldn't be so disappointed if you knew what one of those mother-loving things was like," Carter continued. "They send you so far away that it takes practically an archaeological expedition from Harvard to bring you back."

"I'm sure it's hell, Carter," Rand heard himself say inadequately.

"Thank you, Mr. Mans," he said, leering. "I is real glayud to heah they is still pity left in de human pump."

It's his screwy mockery that gets me, Rand was thinking. I always have to play it straight, and of course he loves my discomfort. "Did they say when you would be coming out?"

"They wouldn't say even if they knew. They're too cagey, it might incriminate them if something went wrong with me and I had to stay longer. I might point my finger at them and say, 'You dirty old liars! You broke your promise to a growing boy.'"

"It isn't such a bad place, is it? I mean, they treat you all right and the food is good, and there are all kinds of facilities for doing one thing and another."

Carter examined him closely, trying to determine if Rand was joking with him. "No, it isn't bad that way," he said thoughtfully. "I could get used to it—in fact, *you* could probably get used to it. Why don't you sign in for a bit? Afraid they wouldn't ever let you out?"

Then he laughed ferociously, and slapped Rand on the knee. "That's all this place needs, you. That would be it." And he laughed on. "Yes indeed. We might turn the place into a new kind of Athens—a very advanced center of creativity and culture. Find your sanity among the insane, brethren. What a fine motto."

Rand was beginning to feel bothered, out of place and therefore vulnerable. The place is for insane people, he was saying to himself, and they're one up on you. They make you feel like a performer of some sort. They bully you, the way Carter is bullying me into placating him and being on the defensive. I never treated him this way—so Japanesey—when he was like the rest of us.

They walked away now, at Rand's subtle unspoken lead, toward the building. He sensed it was getting near departure time, and then *clang! clang!* the bell did ring. And they, like the other dreamy figures on this insane landscape, responded to it, increased their pace to the building. On the knolls and in the glens of green the other figures, green-clad and black, were moving in the same direction, soundlessly and seemingly effortlessly pulled, or propelled, by the same obedient necessity.

"Pavlov," Carter said abruptly, with his new, institution smile, looking at the way they were all responding to the bell.

"But you're not slobbering."

"Give me time. Would you like to see me slobber?"

"Not especially, but if you want to—"

"You're so kind to me, it's killing."

He'll be in for a while yet, Rand was thinking, watching the building come closer and already thinking about the maddening subway ride back into the city.

At the entrance, before good-by, Carter turned to him and said sternly, "One of these days I'd like to get all the fascinating details of how and why I'm in this place. All I know is I didn't sign myself in. I was brought here by Janine and you, presumably because I blew my stack."

"You know what happened," Rand said.

"Yes, I know what you two plus the doctors say, but I still want the facts."

Rand shrugged. This was characteristic of Carter. "Okay," he said. "It was all a plot to get rid of you, right?"

"At least I want to know the exact facts. You don't mind, do you? Just a few teeny-weeny facts for a poor mad creature."

"There are no secrets."

Turning to go, Carter said, finally, "Have you seen Janine lately?"

"Last week, just before she came here."

"You two having a good time?"

"I don't get it."

"You mean you aren't sleeping with her? Come

now," and Carter smiled, "a tasty little brisket like that?"

"Oh for God's sake," and Rand started to go.

"Take it easy," Carter called after him. "Are you coming up next week?"

"Yes, at night. Can I bring you something?"

"Like grapes or a Baby Ruth bar?"

"Oh go to hell," Rand called back jokingly, and walked rapidly toward the gate and guardhouse, weaving in and out of the obedient oncoming green figures and the relieved retreating figures in black and brown and other colors of the street. There were no nurses this time to delight the eye and spring the fantasy. But he was having dinner with Janine so there was no need of this, unless he wanted the whole business even more bewildered than it already was.

Carter was tasting the roast breast of veal that sullenly lingered in his mouth from dinner and looking into the recreation-room bookshelves for something to kill the rest of the night with. He dislodged a trapped shred of the meat, and was holding it on his tongue when he spotted the title of a book that seemed especially fake and disgusting to him. In spontaneous loathing he spit the bit of meat at the book and walked away from the shelves.

"Excrement," he said aloud, and smiled at one of

the other members of his ward, who nodded back very
wisely.

"Precisely."

It was Groz, softly padding up behind him.

"Are you following me again?" Carter asked him.

"Tell me something," Groz went on, ignoring the
question. "Do you think you could ever love me?"

Carter sighed. Groz had never looked more like a
debauched dachshund than he did right now. "All
right," he said wearily, "I'll go through this routine
just once more, Groz, but it's the last time." He began
reciting what Groz wanted to hear: "No, I-could-
never-love-you-not-in-a-million-years."

"Why?"

"Because you are loathsome scum, Groz. You are
a contamination, a stench in the nostrils of my imagi-
nation. You are inconceivably abominable, you are
not even worth micturating on."

"Do other people feel this way about me?"

"Yes, everybody. Everybody I have ever seen in
my life feels this about you. Everybody in the whole
wide world. Every morning four hundred million
Chinese spit on your image to start the day off right."
Carter recited as he had done so many times before.

Now a whimper came into Groz's voice. "Do you
hate me enough to beat me up?"

"To utterly rip you to pieces," said Carter.

Groz was visibly flushing with emotion.

"Well, why don't you?" he whispered with barely repressed desire. "Why don't you rip me to pieces then?"

This was the end of the act, and this was all Carter could submit to.

"Beat it now, Groz. You got what you wanted."

"But you're always saying you're going to do things to me but you never do," he mewed.

"Please, run along, will you? If you're a real nice boy maybe one of these days I'll bash your head in. How's that?"

Groz shook his head sadly. "Empty promises."

Carter left him standing there and strode through the large recreation room, crowded with the green-clad, strangely talking, strangely silent patients, and down the corridor to his room. Or *their room*—himself, and Groz, and the colored boy Bone Livingston —they shared it, an unforgiving iron bed for each tormented body. The walls were bare, undecorated, (just like the brain) except for one picture, and this picture was above Carter's bed, and it was a color portrait of Jesus Christ our Savior, born in Bethlehem. Carter had pinned it there when he first came into the hospital. Sometimes he felt very affectionate toward the picture, sometimes hostile, but he never raised his long, restless hand to take it down.

Livingston was lying in his bed. "You know what I'm going to do when I leave this place?" he asked Carter.

"No, what?" Carter replied, sitting down on his own bed and taking a large notebook from under his pillow.

"I'm going to Hollywood," he said dreamily, smiling up at the ceiling. "I'm going to become a great moving-picture actor. I'm going to write my own pictures and pick my own leading ladies, and at this very moment I got a script on the fire for myself and Miss Barbara Stanwyck."

Carter smiled across at him. "That's wonderful, Bone, really wonderful. I'm very glad you're feeling so high today."

Livingston turned from the ceiling and smiled his delight and appreciation across at Carter.

"Now if you'll please excuse me," Carter went on, opening his notebook, "I have a great deal of work to do."

"To be sure," Livingston said, delicately, and returned his doe gaze to the ceiling.

"We'll talk about it some more tomorrow," Carter added guiltily because he would not for anything hurt

Livingston's feelings. Most people didn't have any feelings, so it was impossible to hurt them. But Bone was not of these foul squid.

He began to read a paragraph he had written in his notebook some time ago:

"They won't let me listen to the radio or watch television. Everybody else watched but me, and they waited until this particular event was to be shown because they knew I wanted so much to see it. Then they said no, you can't watch tonight. They have also begun serving me smaller and poorer portions of food, while the others at the table continue to eat as before. The next time Janine comes I'll tell her to get in touch with the Superintendent immediately and find out why they are discriminating against me. I'm sure they love to treat people this way, and then they tell you it's the therapy.

"Another thing—those goddamn sadistic attendants laugh when they give me shock. Just as I was coming to from one, while they thought I was still out, I heard them laughing and talking about me. One of these days I'm going to kill one of them, that will teach them, the sissy sadistic bastards."

Reading, he had a puzzled reaction to this aspect of himself, or to the experience, because it was not quite the way he felt, or was, at this time, at this moment.

Now for the present. He turned to the last entry in the notebook and began to write.

"Sometimes it is actually like being on a tightrope, and I am not sure of my balance; there is a certain real dizziness and I have the impression that whoever I am around senses this and is waiting for me to fall down, or do something else that would indicate loss of equilibrium. At this point I have to tell myself to come down, or calm down, and then the motors in me slowly purr with less speed. I suppose this is a manifestation of insanity and proof that I really do need help. If it is, then I shall accept it; if I am crazy, then I am crazy and I must recognize the dignity of it.

"I must not lie to myself and others and say I am not, I must not seem ashamed to undergo a natural human phenomenon. It has its own validity, this craziness, and must be treated with respect, like a stranger come to the door asking for directions. Courtesy at least. Who says you have to let him sleep with your wife?

"My wife? How can I tell Janine that I like it here, that I don't particularly want to leave and return to the house with her? And I think she would be a liar to say she is not glad I'm in here. She's getting a rest, which is exactly what I'm getting. What am I going to say to her when I do finally get out (or am thrown out)? And what about Rand? I can't decide whether he is or isn't making love to Janine (assuming that I care).

"Rand, oh what a sly one he is! He reminds me of myself in so many ways. Why do I. . . ."

The lights went out. It was official bedtime.

Go to sleep!

"Didn't Margaret say she was coming?" Roberta Johns asked her husband, about an hour after most of the others had arrived at their apartment.

"Yes, she promised," her husband answered. Obviously it meant something to him. A tweet-tweet of a man.

"She's always late," Roberta went on apprehensively. But the bell at the door yanked her away. It was Rand and he was alone. Roberta took his coat and Mr. Johns almost immediately handed him a highball and steered him into the living room where the others were gathered partying. Janine was already there, and Rand nodded to her and made a point of sitting at the other end of the room. Guilt, but discretion too.

Margaret, meanwhile, was lighting another cigarette in the front seat of her Packard convertible (a most toney collector's item) and wondering how much longer it would be before the young tough on the corner made up his mind to come over to her car.

This was what she was obviously waiting there for,
and he had been shifting from leg to leg for
half an hour, in front of the candy store, but his
courage had not yet risen to the level of his compre-
hension. Maybe it was a cop trap, he might be thinking.

Margaret dragged deeply on her cigarette and
waited patiently. The wait in itself was a zestful part
of what she was doing and she had been vibrating
pleasurably with every moment. For a second she
thought about where she was supposed to be—at the
party with the others. Ah, but this part of her was just
as real as the part that was going to go to the party,
an equal part demanding its full rights.

Suddenly the boy was sauntering to her car, hands
hidden fearfully in pants pockets. He put his head
down to the open window. "Do you know what time
it is, lady?" he inquired, smiling with the knowledge
of the formality of the game.

"Late," Margaret said, opening the door. "Get in."
"*Get in?* Right!"

In ten minutes he was back where he started, getting
out of Margaret's car. She had put the whole thing
to him quite bluntly (this crudeness too being a nuance
of what was happening with her). And he had agreed
to it; in fact, enthusiastically so.

"At nine then," Margaret said when he closed the
door.

"Got you," he replied, grinning lewdly back at her,
and with his thumb and forefinger made a circle to
indicate total agreement and understanding.

"Fine," and she started the car up.

The boy would bring the girl to her place tomorrow
night at nine and they were to get twenty dollars each.
For less than an evening's work, quite good pay when
you looked at it from their direction. Now she sped
uptown on the East River Drive to the Johnses' apartment. Very pleased, very relieved.

Just like a child, she was thinking of the boy. His
name was Joey and the girl's name Nina. He had
volunteered this last name in the rise of his newly
perverted enthusiasm.

Until now this day had been a blighted one, begun
in sorrow at being alone and carried on throughout
the headlong hours by self-hatred and despair. She
did not even know where to go. (Besides the Johnses'
place tonight, but that was not *going* as she needed or
meant it.)

Then, driving through the fevered, quietly depraved
East Side, she saw the handsome young tough, after
seeing, on many corners, the tight-figured arrogant
young girl beauties, his counterparts, and that had

restored her vitality and interest. She had done this once before, six months ago, an inspiration right out of the blue sky, and it had gone off most satisfyingly.

Through the open window blew the river smell, bloodlike yet sordidly pungent too, strongly alive and also refuse-like dead, and quite immediately it became the odor enclosing her and Joey and Nina as they would all three be, their special complex fragrance. *Oh! Oh!* For seconds Margaret ached sweetly.

She drove away now from the river section, leaving behind all that throbbing promise, and toward the area of the Johnses' social gathering, several blocks west, with its totally opposite penumbra and magnetism, and her thoughts and attitudes and imminent behavior, like ingratiating schoolboys who know which side their bread is buttered on, began to arrange themselves, accordingly, in familiar patterns.

The Wandering Jew, Phillips mused as he stepped off the bus and began sloping toward the Johnses' upper-class building, I wonder if that's what I am. Peeking into the nooks and neuroses of this panting world. Seeking what? Pleasure? Love? Money? Pain? What? He suddenly had to laugh. Life! That's what I'm seeking, all that great apple pie of existence. What other quest is there? Tell me that, old Dog

Star up there. You got something better up your
sleeve? He breathed deeply. A great night for man
and especially beast. For just a depressing moment,
he recalled Monday—unsuccessfully looking for a
job in a couple of publishing houses. Ugh! He made
himself think of something else—the Johnses' party
and all the goodies awaiting him there. Live on the
fatheads of the land, that's what I'd do if I were really
smart, people like the Johnses who have no *raison
d'etre*. Ah, what's it like to be a well-heeled zero
whose only thought of the morrow is whether your
soft-boiled eggs will be too dribbly, or whether the
little wifey will stop complaining of headaches just
when a man's sails are set? Must be great for a while.
Wonder if old Harry will be here tonight. He smiled.
That wild Harry—one of the few people left in this
city whom one can really talk to. Writes lies for an
advertising agency, but certainly manages to keep
the old belfry in sound order. Haven't seen much of
him lately . . . drifted apart. But that's the way it
seems to go with nearly everybody I know. Armpit
buddies one day, sly-eyed strangers the next. Why?
Nothing stable in the human heart, or something.

Just then he saw Margaret step out of her car and
stride briskly toward the apartment-building entrance.

Yoicks! It's the hound of the Baskervilles herself!
And he crossed himself.

2
5

"SOMETHING'S HAUNTING HIM," said Roberta Johns of Rand after he had brushed by her on his way to the kitchen.

"What?"

"I said something's. . . ."

"No, I meant *what* is haunting him? I heard. . . ."

"I really don't know, to tell you the truth. He's so *restless.*"

"Excellent party," her companion said. He was a tall, bearded Negro, and he had known Mrs. Johns only shortly. He was quite sober.

"Hmm," was Roberta's reply.

How shall I break away? she was wondering. He keeps clinging to me like a terrified little girl. How . . . "Oh, excuse me," seeing a face floating around by itself, "I *must* talk to that person," and she fled.

Didn't fool me, he thought, turning elsewhere, high-ball to his beard. But he was still pleased to be here, among these people, and fathoms within himself he sighed philosophically. Never look a gift horse in its moated eye, that much he knew. He also knew he probably should have contempt for this attitude, but he couldn't muster it. Just not in him, unfortunately. Sometimes he found himself wistfully wishing he could afford real contempt for things around him. A few minutes ago he was manufacturing conversation with a fastidiously dressed couple—named what?— who insisted on being so overanxiously decent and "liberated" with him—"Isn't it simply *destestable* the way the middle class still regards mixed marriages!"—that he thought he was going to come down with a severe case of whistling hives right then and there. But he had grinned instead. Easier.

In a near corner he saw two people he wished to know—Rand and Harry, whom he had heard mentioned during the party—but he was too timid to approach them just like that, so he stayed where he was, a tiny black satellite, he felt, suspended in cold white space, and listened in on their prized conversation.

"Rocky, or Assault, or Deception—that's what I'd name a son if I had one," Harry was telling Rand.

"Why?"

"Because it would be more contemporary and realistic. A name like that would start him off on the right foot. Christ, can you imagine saddling a kid in the atomic age with a monicker like Lucian or Bobby?"

Rand had to laugh. Funny bastard, Harry.

"And first off, I'd teach him the value of money and how to lie."

Harry grinned angelically.

Then Rand said, "You know, you use your mind like a hand grenade."

Harry's face was wreathed with pleasure.

"What a delicious line! But," he added, "all iambic pentameter aside, what do you mean?"

"I mean you purposely throw your mind into a group of people, a conversation, hoping to hit everybody with a little fragment, hoping to draw blood."

"Well?"

"Well nothing."

"You know what your trouble is?" Harry began, putting an avuncular hand on Rand's arm. "You're too nice, and that's bad. Let me give you a morsel of advice."

The bearded Negro strained his delicately shaped ears a point beyond their normal range.

"Go on," Rand said. He respected Harry, he would listen to him this way.

"Try to stop thinking in absolutes. It can give you lockjaw."

"What's that got to do with being nice?"

"A lot," continued Harry. "Just think about it. There's a kind of motivating absolutism about niceness. Gives me the creeps, to tell you the truth."

"What's wrong with being nice?"

"Nothing, if you don't carry it too far. But that's not really what I'm talking about. I mean your philosophy of niceness. It isn't relevant to modern life. Niceness is sick, neurotic, and not, as you seem to think, 'human.' "

There was a good deal of party noise all over, laughter and loud talking and a collective vibration, like something coming out of an electric machine. In a distant corner Phillips was caressing a beautiful young girl on a divan. Rand, mulling over what Harry had said, watched him for a second, turned away, saw the bearded Negro satellite suspended nearby.

So did Harry.

"Who's the Babylonian?" he asked Rand.

Negro winces.

"He writes."

"They all seem to, these days. It's a new form of slavery."

The Negro still wanted to meet them, but was too timid, and he couldn't budge from this orbit, those awful eyes upon him.

"I think he heard you," remarked Rand softly, taking his eyes off the man.

"Why is he listening to us then? His legs aren't broken."

The poor guy, thought Rand of the Negro. He did not want to venture into the subject any further; that is, pathetic people, because he well knew Harry's feeling therein. A shark among carp.

Elsewhere in the big room Janine held her high-ball glass with both hands resting in her lap like a half-lost traveler brought in out of the snow and handed a warming glass of grog. Shyly looked across the room at Rand (he's sweet), then hurriedly looked away when she thought she was observed in this by Roberta Johns. Caught? No, just my guilt. If Carter were here, as of old, she would be tense with anger and embarrassment because he would be tight and belligerently arguing with someone, anyone, or else clumsily making a pass at any likely woman. Or accusing her of being a depressing clam with no sort of zip, which according to him he very much required. Should have joined a circus then. Why is it that I don't feel like participating in these things anymore? she asked herself, sipping her drink.

"I do wish you'd stay here with us for a while, dear," Roberta was saying. "And let us take care of you."

"It's all right," Janine heard herself reply. I'll have to learn to be alone." I don't believe a word of it, but I couldn't help saying it. I'm becoming a hypocrite.

"I know *exactly* how you feel, Jan darling," Roberta murmured quite seriously, pressing her hand. "Exactly."

Elsewhere, "What was that you were telling me the other day about exploiting schizophrenia?" Rand asked Harry.

Flattered, Harry smiled.

"Oh that. Well, instead of destroying yourself with anxiety by repressing certain aspects of your whole self, aspects that conflict with the so-called moral self, why, it would be better to try to express them all. For example, if you have some criminal desires, become a part-time thief, or at least let the emotion have some badly needed exercise. See what I mean?"

Rand thought he did. This Harry was so stimulating but so confusing. Take him seriously? Just how activate such an idea as his?

"Chaos," he said aloud.

"No. A completely new form of freedom. 'Give yourself a break'—that should be a maxim for our time."

Harry's gaze now wandered, lit again on the Negro, but shifted, fell upon Phillips.

"Look at Phillips sniff that redhead, just *look* at him."

(And the Negro, of course, looked too.)

"Honey," Phillips was murmuring, "you turn me into a huge jelly of love, you know that?" touching her ear with his nose tip.

"Do I? It sounds disgusting."

"No, it's wonderful, completely wonderful, and I'm grateful to you. Why don't we leave soon?" More ear-lobe nosing.

"Will you teach me how to play tennis?" the girl asked.

"This very night. Now shall we leave?"

"Well, in a minute. Let's stay for just one more drink."

He moaned impatiently, nose tip probing into ear.

"Revolting!"

"Who?"

"Him," said Margaret, pointing her finger at Phillips. "He has no sense of dignity at all."

Her friend, a balding man within a stone's throw of middle age, shrugged. "How can you be dignified with a girl that pretty? And who would want to be?"

Phillips and the redhaired girl were leaving, Phillips holding her small white hand as though it were a rare and fragile flower just carried in from the forests by native runner.

"Do you know him?" the man asked Margaret.

"Quite well. We were lovers once."

"*Oh*, I *see*."

"Do you? Because *I* don't."

She watched Phillips leave, then in the same gaze she saw the bearded Negro approaching, passing Phillips, seemingly headed toward the vacant seat on the couch, next to her. Inexorably he came on and on.

"Pardon me, but is anyone sitting here?"

Is he English? That accent. Not with the face but with the beard, well yes. "No, sit down." Homosexual? That would of course explain it. But that would be too easy. Imitation of a pansy? Perhaps, perhaps. But then why? Why mime a queer?

"Can I get you a drink?" he suggested urgently.

"No thanks. But—and she watched for the shock this would produce—"I will take a sip from yours if I may."

"Quite a combination," said Rand, looking at the Negro and Margaret. "Don't you think?"

"Even Rimbaud couldn't have dreamed it up," cracked Harry. "But I like her."

"So do I. It's just that she's kind of spooky."

Should I go over and say a few words to Janine? Harry wondered, looking about. Could I really *say* something to the mousy little thing, or would it be

all empty mockery? And would it matter to her? But
she's flanked by those two grinning mongoloids. Bet
they're talking about one of the arts. Ugh. Culture,
how I despise it! What was it the man said?—"When
I hear the word culture, I draw out my revolver."
Sometimes I wish I were a cop. I'll wait till later to
see her. Dart across no man's land when nobody's
peeking.

Rand saw Robert Johns coming out of the kitchen
holding high an immense tray loaded with several
varieties of cold meats and cheeses and other late-hour
savories. He had, a moment ago, felt like leaving, for
he had seen everyone he wanted to see but now he
reversed himself and decided, in sensitive obligation
to the approaching tray, that he was quite hungry.

Harry was thinking and surveying and watching
himself cavort upon the stage of disintegrating contemporary history. I hold a stale drink that I met years
ago sitting on a studio floor next to twenty years of
jazz, and it's been popping up in my life ever since,
like a crazy creditor. I've come to this party loaded
down with all the paraphernalia of my trade as a
human being, including several hundred different
psychic disguises and costumes. Each disguise and
costume is fitted tightly over the other, and I feel like
a huge artichoke.

The hostess, an unreformed vampire, now drags me
over to a crowd-pleasing heavyweight literary critic
who, as I arrive, has just finished outboxing Tolstoi.
The world is not big enough for both him and literature. He's trying for a KO over it.

I sit down in my ringside seat, feeling Schenley's
palsy creep over me, and watch this man, who is a
little slow on his feet but a terrific puncher, beat the
hell out of three young poets and a minor English
novelist who, he proves, does not know a double image
from a rat hole. In the intermission before the main
event, I manage to beguile a neighbor with a couple
of my disguises and psychic labyrinths. But then the
bell rings for the big fight, with Cervantes. I stumble
away, punchdrunk and frustrated.

It seems I've been standing and sitting and leaning
now for days, howling and laughing and glooming but
still waiting the chance for my own great act. I suddenly realize that for several minutes an old acquaintance has been shaking my hand and discussing one of
his stock personal problems. He has a grip like vice
but he doesn't know it. He's telling me a spectacular
story about how he once sabotaged himself as a child.
I gently throw him over my shoulder by saying that I
have to make wee wee.

I spy a shrill group around a clown who lives in

reproduction. This man progresses through life back-first. I listen to him shout about something that happened to him two weeks ago. It has taken him this long to react to what happened. He must have time to give reality a false but digestible form, to imagine himself as the victor or the abject loser in a particular situation, and in this way he controls reality. The lie and the revaluation are his specialities. Nothing will happen to him tonight. It will happen yesterday, or the day before. He is the man who in his analyst's office likes to describe himself as "he."

I grope my way into another corner where someone is stentoriously giving a speech that is thinly disguised as conversation. I listen to them—or him—thinking I might wedge in my act here. This madman is discussing something very intimate, like a recent love scene, but he makes it sound like Prescott's *Conquest of Peru*. It's his way of talking. He uses language as a means of excommunication. Now he laughs, and as I turn my head sadly away I hear his laughter echoing through hundreds of empty rooms.

Near my right elbow is an intellectual striptease giving a show. He had displayed everything he has ever known and thought; and now determined to please still further, he seems to be on the verge of disemboweling himself. I can't stay to watch this.

Something brushes by my leg. It's a rare and recent organism who is gliding in and out of various gatherings. He is something between the orchid and the hermit crab. He is a Nood. His life activity is moving in, anywhere, after the foundation has already been laid. Now he pauses to overhear someone tell his emotional reaction to a recent movie. A smile sneaks over the Nood's face. He is already assuming this other person's emotional reaction, making it his very own, and I can see him putting on his slippers and lighting up his pipe. Suddenly he scuttles off to another human cluster. Over there a theory is being born for which he has long had several practical applications, waiting for the ground to be broken.

I fumble over to several part-time teachers, reviewers, etcetera, who are trying to shout each other down with their parodies of normality. They compare their simple naturalistic routines. One states dogmatically that he hasn't read a book since childhood. Another screams that all he does all day long is play pitch-penny with the kids on the corner. Just a bunch of regular fellows. Not an alienated man among them. I hack my way out of this luxuriant growth of mediocrity and head for what looks like a nice cool plateau.

On the plateau several people are lying about in

statue-like positions. They have been trying to see
who was the coolest, by the length of time they would
refuse to speak to each other. Three of them are so
cool they have frozen to death in this hip silence. Two
are turning to stone. Not a word has been spoken, not
a gesture risked in hours. I flee this deep freeze, frost-
bitten.

Have knocked over two young jerks and got next to
a model. She is perfection. The way she walks, her
gestures, the movement of her mouth, her conversation, her clothes, everything absolutely stylized,
synchronized toward the same end—airtightness. Airtightness so that nothing can penetrate her; within its
aura nothing unpleasant can happen. Volcanoes ex-
plode with an apologetic murmur, tragedy removes
itself a thousand miles.

Tired, confused, helpless, I retreat from the front
lines back to the kitchen where I begin to mix myself
a drink. But two young men block my way to the ice-
box. They're exchanging folio after folio of baroque
clichés in a soft, effeminate plot against meaning.
One raises his eyebrow chicly and murmurs Marlene,
and in that moment an obscene pact has been signed.

One final look before I run. The place is a shambles.
Groans, writhings, new inner Saharas discovered,
threatened leaps. Horrible.

"What do you think made Carter go off his chump?" Harry inquired, now returned from his fantasy, as he reached for more liverwurst and rye.

"Just about everything, I guess," answered Rand, and took some ham and pumpernickel, hoping that Roberta was pleased by this because he truthfully was not in the least bit hungry. "Couldn't stand himself any longer."

"I always thought he would flip. It certainly figured."

"We might all do it one of these days."

"We already have, *liebchen*. And don't you forget it."

3

JANINE AND RAND were strolling in the park, arm linked in hopeful arm, and Janine cried abruptly, "But it isn't fair to him!"

"I know," Rand replied, his eyes awed by the bloody-looking fall leaves. "But what's so fair about going insane? To you, I mean." He turned to her. "I'm not being facetious. There are a lot of people who don't go insane, because of certain deeply experienced responsibilities, like a family. When he did that, he gave you up—or rather forsook you. Remember, *he's* being taken care of completely, body and soul, and by specialists in both fields."

"I still feel guilty."

"There's nothing wrong, per se, with feeling guilty. But you should find out why you feel guilty."

"You," she said almost delicately.

"*Me?* What in God's name have I done, whom

have I betrayed? Liking you, seeing you, wanting you,
yet not consummated to date—no, I'm sorry, I'm no
monster, nor are you. Sorry."

"Oh! He's still being deceived."

"Besides which by your own admission you aren't
even sure you want to be loyal to him."

"I know! I know! Oh, I'm so confused, God!" and
her arm drew his toward her for support of some
kind.

"Plotinus knew what he was talking about," he remarked, returning his gaze to the rioting fall blood.
But which *am* I doing here? he wondered. Falling in
love with this girl, or taking care of *his* wife because
I think I owe it to him, like somebody administering
an anesthetic, or feeding a cat during a vacation?
Guilty? Christ, I'm the one wallowing in guilt.

"He suspects something," she said, "but of course
it could be merely his general paranoia."

Suddenly they were at the lake, a precipice
dropping right in front of them, sheerly, and this,
perversely, made the lake doubly smooth and tranquil, almost stagey it seemed and the black dots,
which were small ducks, premeditated.

"Paranoia," he repeated after her. "It sounds like
an idyllic noun, or a mountain flower. In this context
—the lake, the pure precipice, the blood-red leaves,

the ducks—it sounds poetic and desirable. Don't you think so?"

Now she laughed, a phenomenon she had not released all afternoon.

"Yes, it does."

And so the long kiss (it was their very first) that immediately, quite naturally followed, was very sweet and needed, in this bloody-leaved, sheer-precipiced nature setting, and no guilt coursed through him as he pressed her small-breasted, warm-smelling body to his, even though, for half a moment, he did see Carter's tortured face staring into his (but not necessarily accusingly) from somewhere among the inflamed treetops. Ahoy!

She tastes so different from her whom I hate— my own dear Xantippe, who is a bitter herb both to my figurative and literal taste buds. What's she doing right now? Shopping for a new stiletto? And as for me, I should be looking for a job, a grindstone to put my proboscis to.

"What does all this mean?" Janine asked him shyly.

"I don't honestly know. All we can do is wait and find out."

Harry examined himself once more in the old-fashioned bureau mirror, to be sure that no trace of his other self was there evident. Loud tie, draped suit, vulgar, ready expression—no, nothing showed through this brilliant façade. The other Harry was successfully left behind, downtown with his wife who did not have the remotest idea of his biweekly change of character and name and occupation and, in fact, entire life. Here was Mr. Hyde or Dr. Jekyll, whichever you preferred, whichever circle of humans you happened to be in at a given moment, the figure of Harry or Eddie Brien as he was up here in the Bronx—Eddie Brien, photographer's assistant, living alone, who went with some of the boys and a couple of the girls. A kind of part-time neighborhood hanger-on, you might say.

"What do you say, Ace?" he said to his mirrored face in the neighborhood accent, smiling with proper slyness, and then, pleased with himself, went out into the unbelievably filthy neighborhood labyrinths.

In the course of his cagey saunter to the Shannon Bar he began his own brain washing, applied the final touch of magic for the awaiting stage.

The very rhythm of the sly, rat-eyed neighborhood-style walk helped him in this, penetrated to his brain in luring waves, beckoning, beckoning, almost tide-like. Like self-hypnosis, difficult, to be sure, but to the fanatic quite possible. Obscenities began pouring into his mind, and notions of violence (patterns of old driven far out of sight) ; he saw himself in a different image, with different attitudes and desires. It was working gradually.

The Shannon Bar approached, and so did Eddie Brien. A long figure in front watched him come up with a movie-like intensity and silence.

"What you been doing with yourself?" Eddie asked him, grinning dirtily, and giving him a friendly shove.

"Same old crap," his friend Mac said, hands now stuck back in warm pockets. He was cold and looked it (his eyes had a mackerel numbness) but still he could not think his way inside the warm bar.

Eddie grabbed his arm. "Come on, I'll stand you to a beer."

The other guffawed. "You crazy or something?"

"Yeah, that's it. I'm batty."

The bar was darkish and drunken and contained the promise of becoming disorderly; it felt of violence just beneath the soiled skin. The jukebox cut into the smoky air with its hallucinated screaming. Eddie pushed into a place at the bar, between two bleared Irish laborers, and yelled for the beers, feeling quite natural about it. At home.

"Guess who's sitting over there," Mac said suddenly.

"Who?"

"Shanley, and the bastard has two pieces with him. *Two!*" And his voice rose in an agony of unbelief.

They moved quickly, and in a matter of seconds Shanley (acne-scarred small face) was saying, "And this is an acquaintance of mine named Eddie Brien. Eddie, meet Miss Myra Gotch on my right and Edna Lee directly across from me."

"Pleased to meet you."

"Likewise," one piece said, while the other smiled and nodded, voiceless.

They were twin-like in their pert, tight-fitting beauty and skein of slight hardness (just slight, though), and they were young. Eddie sat next to the free one, and she did not mind at all that almost immediately he pressed his thigh against hers and inquired as to where he might purchase a sweater like the one she was now wearing. They all laughed as she did at the joke.

After a few beers (during which Mac cruelly kept cracking his poor knuckles), Shanley, a trucker's helper who lived with his Irish peasant parents and retarded sister, was leaning slightly toward Eddie and saying, "Want to make some easy dough?"

"Who said I didn't?"

"Okay." Shanley flicked his eyes to Mac. "You too," he said (which momentarily paused the knuckle cracking). Then he outlined his plan, which also involved the two girls sitting with them.

"How do you know we won't get caught?" Myra hesitantly asked when Shanley had finished describing the scheme.

"What's the matter? You chicken?"

"I didn't say that," she replied, flushed.

"Okay then, you in or not?"

Her reply was quick and ashamed. "Sure I am. I'm in."

Eddie liked her, liked her embarrassment and ready toughness. Under the table her leg felt warm and inviting. This was very much for him. He moved his arm in such a way as to brush against her breast, and he felt her slight tremor of coy pleasure.

"Let's blow this dump and go dancing," he said authoritatively. He was beer-bloated, and that was a dumb feeling. Elsewhere on his emotional scale he felt another tremor, over Shanley's clever money-making scheme; it had an almost touchable aesthetic immediacy.

"Yeah," said Mac. "This goddamn stuff is floating my back teeth."

The girls giggled and they all struggled up to leave.

"Wait," said Myra. "I've got to go," and she minced tightly back to the ladies' room.

This was contagious.

"Me too," the other remarked happily, and she skipped urgently away.

"Nice, huh?" Shanley ventured rhetorically as the three men watched the girls high-heeling it into the staling farness of the bar.

For reply Eddie merely, but loudly, smacked his lips. Eddie and Edna. Yes, oh yes indeedy.

We live in a time of extreme devices, he'd once told someone. Applied to himself as well as all those other coagulated blobs out there. For was not this programmatic double identity the most extreme device of all? But he had to do it, absolutely no way out. Only way he could save himself for himself. The other way, the death way, was to be the good boy they wanted you to be. Oh the foulness of it! Wanted to turn you into a cultural fag, when all's said and done. Oh the harm they've perpetrated, the generations they've murdered with their culture straitjackets! You'll never know what *real* poets have died unseen, unsung. How the blobs hate life! Worshipers of darkness, all of them. How did the whole perverted thing get started, anyway? Who was the first corrupter of humankind's future? Life, life, there's nothing like it. Burn the goddamn books. Start all over again. Up with Eddie Brien! For he shall lead you. Onward!

Today Janine told Carter how it all happened: it
had seemed to Carter that he was listening to a fright-
ening story about someone else whom he felt he knew
but at a distressing distance (as on a storm-stricken
terrain where forms are bathed in gentle amber lights
of anxiety distortion), and this made the story doubly
grotesque, as though he had the identity of the person
on the tip of his tongue but it obstinately, or, fiend-
ishly, refused to slither off.

"I didn't know anything was wrong," she said,
"until you began to drive fast. You remember—no, I
guess not—anyway, we were coming back from a
weekend in the country at the Stones' and you had
drunk a lot at lunch, despite the fact that I begged
you not to. You had acted sort of loud then, or frantic,
but it seemed like your usual self with a few drinks.
But then on the way back you began to drive very fast,
passing all the cars as though you didn't see them, and
I was afraid we were going to have a wreck. You got
up to eighty miles an hour. When I pleaded with you
to slow down, that the police might get us, you just
laughed and said 'I might get them!' When I said I
didn't understand, you said, 'That's because you
don't understand God, or me, or any of these similar
high matters.' Then I knew you were sick, not only
drunk, and I wanted to die it was such an awful
realization. Oh God it was so awful.

"After that—you kept smiling all the time—you began to say all sorts of things. That the homosexuals were not going to take over the world because you weren't going to let them, and that any weakling could be a homo today, it was the easy way out. You also said something about our going to South Africa to start a new life. It frightened me terribly, all of it, and you continued driving as fast as you could. I tried not to listen to all you said but I couldn't stop it, and there was nothing I could think of to say to you either.

"When we got home you began to make speeches about everything, and I called a psychiatrist friend of my sister's to come to see you. He did, and said you should be committed and given shock treatments, that you had suffered a serious breakdown. Paranoia, he said. So we brought you here."

"Where was Rand?" he had asked.

"Rand! He wasn't anywhere."

"You mean he wasn't around with you and the psychiatrist when I was locked up?"

"No, of course not. I called him later. After all, he was your closest friend. Why shouldn't I have called him?"

Could that be the truth or was it another of their weird lies? he wondered, now that Janine was gone and he was sitting in the big recreation room (the iron bars on the windows casting apologetic shadows across his face), more or less sparsely surrounded by the somnambulist, ballet-posing, green-clad loons. Didn't remember any of that back there, at all, thank you very much, Mr. Shock Machine, and I hope I can do as much for you sometime. But he did remember now, of what *was* before, and partner to the memory (really what seemed to be leading the memory in by its hesitant little hand), was a crushing ennui-distaste for it.

O God Almighty! No! Sorry but I'm afraid you have to, old chap. Rules of the game and all that, you know. The blank pea-green recreation room wall before him was the blank wall of his mind onto which was now projected what he could remember of what happened for a while prior to the Fall. Insatiable amount of drinking and furious emotional explosions with Janine and with friends, the guilt of it utterly inundating him for days afterward in his spent condition.

Before his eyes a mammoth image appeared . . . he was beating Janine up in their bathroom because she had accused him of sleeping with someone, which he denied but which he had done (oh please take it away, forgive me), but who had it been? Who? Oh, with Phillips he had been part of that night.

"Queer for old biddies!" he suddenly said aloud

(startled, like a crane at feeding, a green-clad figure suddenly looked across at him (as it came back, focused, and was now there on the screen before him:

It had been at the house of a Mrs. Freda Haller. He had compulsively ended up there after a demonic drunken voyage from place to place, because he slightly knew Mrs. Haller, something of a wealthy woman with a cultural interest, and in her late forties (very gentle, her face now seemed, on the wall). And of all people, who was there but Phillips, not exactly in bed but certainly hovering about in that thought zone. And he had drunkenly insulted him about something—what? his work? his clothes? what? his job? Oh Jesus! Poor Phillips, poor old Phillips having to experience that obnoxious evening. (He now re-called, in mitigation, writing him a faintly cringing note of apology next day.)

The happy bruised face of Groz suddenly passed in front of him, with a triumphantly blackened eye, made a shadow on his screen, passed on, as the projection resumed its whirring, irrevocably bigger-than-life images of the past.

Once the awful void had opened, back there before he wound up in here, it leeringly refused to close, and, lemming-like, he could not reverse his own speed. The awful void being the realization that he no longer

contained his own center of reality and must, therefore, conduct his search on the *outside*, not inside
himself, as is proper. That sort of thing can lead to
almost anything, which is exactly what it did. He tried
quite fervently to *drum up* experience. Anything from
draining various bars to screwing various women to
omniverously gobbling up information from people
about themselves. "And then what did you do?" "Gee,
Carter, you want to know everything, don't you?"
"Oh come on. Stop being coy. Tell me the rest of the
story." As though he had a cuff big enough to write a
novel on. Gimme gimme gimme.

Whir on, bright past, whir on.

Now he saw himself screaming at Janine.

"You're a drag, goddamn it! You never want to do
anything anymore. I'm dying of boredom because of
you."

"That's right. Blame it on me. It's simpler that way.
If you're so eager for something to happen, go on
out and make it happen. I'll sit this one out."

"Just like you, kiddo. Why don't you go back to
Pago Pago?"

Five telephone calls (*Help! help! Man drowning!*),
and, through a friend of Phillips he managed to find
himself a place to go. The house of a middle-aged
German couple, well-heeled and deliciously urbane

and worldly. They had, it seemed, run the gamut a couple of times and this night, Carter was delighted to discover, they were embarking on their third journey, with him as traveling tourist.

"Have you ever played Confession, Mr. Barrows?" our hostess inquired (they were hitting the sauce in earnest now).

"No, but I certainly would love to sometime," said Carter, grinning.

An English girl was present besides the friend of Phillips. Nice.

"Splendid. We'll play it now. It goes this way: we take turns guessing each other's big secret and making up a story around it. Exciting, no?"

"Lead me to it."

Her chubby husband grinned at the English girl, like a hungry boar who has just nosed a truffle. They all joined hands, so to speak, and went at it, in fiends' play. The air got thicker, the sauce, into which they were diving, deeper.

I know your secret but you don't know mine! Ya! Ya!

"You once killed a man!"

"You're afraid you can't have a baby!"

"You made love to your own son!"

"You think you're a fraud!"

"You went to jail once for stealing!"

Ya! Ya!

Oodles of fun for a while as long as the secret was not his.

"Let me see," began the fat host, his eyes tigering upon drunk Carter. "I would say that your secret is that you cannot stand to be alone. You are a true coward."

The host paused before presenting his fantasy of Carter's true cowardice. That gave Carter just enough time to jump up and hit the man in the face. Then he rushed drunkenly from the room, shouting:

"You're a bunch of goddamn degenerates!"

The looks on their faces were staring him down now, shaming him with the stupidity of it. Oh Christ, no!

But the vengeful whirring of the past recalled continued.

Margaret was getting herself set for the evening and she was nervously excited. (Had not the Roman emperors done the same sort of thing, for the hungry, restless plebians?) She looked at the large golf-leaf clock on the mantel: it was nearly time. She began to mix herself another drink, her sixth, when the telephone rang.

Oh! something's gone wrong, she thought with panic, and ran unhappily across the large baroque room to the telephone table. She barely made herself whisper hello.

"Oh! It's you!" she shouted angrily into the bearded Negro's ear (and why not? for this was *their* night—hers and Joey's and Nina's—theirs alone. What right did *he* have to bungle in?)

"I can't talk to you now. I'm having a shower," and she hung up.

"*Having* a shower? Are you getting married?" he inquired into the dead phone.

"*Taking* a shower" she said aloud, but to herself in the middle of the room, smiling at the mistake, relieved though angry at him. Just because he's a Negro he thinks I'm obligated by the fact that he likes me, that he's offering himself to me. But I won't, I'm not, damn him. It isn't that he isn't nice, or as good as anybody else, it's just this insidious assumption of his. . . . obligation . . . white women's burden . . . but I did lead him on, I guess . . . oh dear.

She sank down into the big easy chair (drink back in hand), and back into the luxuriant growth of her expectations for the evening. When *would* they get here? Over the mantel hung a Sargent portrait of her maternal grandmother, and now they examined each other suspiciously.

"Hold onto your hat, dearie," Margaret advised the woman, smiling quite pleasantly.

Doorbell. *Finally.*

"The first thing you dears will want is a drink," she said.

"It's cold outside," the girl said.

"It always is," relied Margaret from the liquor cabinet, and both Joey and Nina laughed in confused appreciation.

She was exactly what Margaret had expected (or hoped for): shy but essentially immune to the opinions or morals of others (purely amoral), heavily made up as she undoubtedly imagined movie stars looked, vulgarly beautiful, in evening dress (what incredible—no, *inspired*—taste!) and could not possible be older than eighteen. Perfectly edible young figure, to say nothing of her perfume.

"Oh! I *love* Scotch and soda," Nina murmured, gazing into the magic-filled glass.

Joey snorted. "What do you mean you *love* Scotch and soda? I bet you never had any before."

"You're crazy," she snapped. Turning to Margaret, "Don't believe anything he says."

"I'll try not to."

Joey snorted again, perhaps at both of them, and began walking around the room looking at everything (as did Nina for abrupt unabashed seconds, but only

with darting eyes) which to him was totally new or
unreal. Margaret watched him: his clothes were so
tight and "elegant," he reminded her suddenly of a
young flamenco dancer in Barcelona, arrogant, proud,
small buttocks . . . the flamenco boy seemingly incor-
ruptible. . . .

"Who's that?"

She was jolted. "Who's who?" Margaret asked the
girl.

"*That*," repeated Nina, pointing to the Sargent
portrait.

"Oh, *that*. Well—that's a picture of a grandmother
of mine."

"Very *nice*."

"I hated her."

"You did?"

Margaret got up. "I have some wonderful records.
Let's hear them, shall we?" She was tight and she
wished they were too. (Had he explained the arrange-
ment to this lovely Nina or was it going to be a violat-
ing surprise?)

Not long after that they were drunk, and in this
condition shy-*seeming* Nina revealed herself to be a
natural-born exhibitionist. This manifested itself first
in the dancing with Joey (who was setting the pace, as
was natural and pre-agreed) : he began, quite expertly

because he did it almost as a formal aspect of the dancing, to play with Nina and she not only did not object or rather react as though something unusual or incongruous were happening, but responded fluidly and brilliantly (still within the framework of the dancing) and contributed improvisations of her very own. Indeed it was a challenging game! Young, unthinking, uncaring, absolutely themselves.

And this was but the beginning. From a certain tacitly felt, magical point on they had almost no conversation, as such. Margaret immersed herself with every feeling and nerve in her role of Watcher, and Nina and Joey immersed themselves with equal abandon in their parts as Performers. Joey danced twice with Margaret, performing his very skilled little tricks, and this was, to be sure, an *addition*, but it was his dancing with Nina that was the whole idea. One dance followed another—one drink more or less keeping a parallel—and progressed in theatrics. Margaret was becoming delirious with her watcher's pleasure.

Their clothes now began to appear in various places in the room, flung suddenly into the air and onto a chair, or dropped delicately onto the rug there at their feet. Nothing in this world could have recalled them now, nothing. Margaret stayed as she was but in her mind of course it was quite different. Then Joey and

Nina were rolling on the floor in front of her, yelling
fierce sexual obscenities at each other, *driven! driven!*
while Margaret managed for the approaching moments to remain watching in the chair, but when the
floor-grappling reached near climax she could no
longer contain the demons in her, and she was there
writhing on the floor next to them, drunkenly ripping
off her own clothes and moaning in high unbearable
pleasure and desperation, now clawing at herself, now
rubbing her face over the contorted face of Nina, over
her body, now kissing Joey's muscular torso, and
sobbing and pleading urgently to both God and Satan
to aid her in this time of awful torment.

"Oh Jesus!" whimpered young Nina in her un-
hampered ecstasy. *"Oh Jesus!"*

The bearded young Negro, Christopher Hawkins,
stopped suddenly and stared at himself in the store-
front mirror. A hawklike nose would do it, he said to
himself. I'd seem Arabian then, but *this* way . . . and
he shook his head. Still mirror-examining (it was
peaceful there, one might say homelike; could float—
yes, why not?—here all day), he thought about Margaret. All that money and nothing to do . . . what's
the matter with her? One day steaming, next day
chilblains.

Challenged one's dignity, that's what it did. That was one of the things he loved about the University. Nobody ever challenged his dignity. He wished he had a photograph of himself—life-size—lecturing to his class, standing there straight and tall and with beautifully authoritative composure. Herr Professor, B.A., M.A., Ph.D.

"The remarkable thing about Shakespeare," Professor Hawkins was intoning to his students, "was his ability, or capacity, to identify himself in his work with so many different types. Most writers can identify with only one character, and that is usually an image of themselves. Hence, however many books they write, they are essentially always writing the same book about the same person."

"Would you say that was because of his great intellectual powers?" asked a devout and respectful young girl student.

"Shakespeare was *not* an intellectual."

"No?"

"Absolutely not," he went on in delicious authority and confidence. "He was a man of quite ordinary tastes, very much of the common people, who had this genius for drama. You don't read Shakespeare for ideas because there simply aren't any."

He coolly watched the class as they let this, to them,

new valuation sink in. He felt splendid as he did so, as though he had just won a hard footrace in a track meet. Proud. *They* knew who he was and they sweetly depended on his sure grasp of things. In his high moments he sometimes let himself feel like their father-surrogate. Which also allowed him to feel that he inspired a slight measure of fear. As it should be. His superior knowledge was the oak staff with which he ruled his young flock. Loved to give them long talks. Just like delivering an edifying sermon. Some sort of self-induced ecstasy.

"Excuse me, Professor Hawkins, but could I drop by your office one of these days soon? I've written something which I'd very much appreciate having you look at." "A pleasure, Brown. Come ahead."

The tight white face of Rand now suddenly passed his, and he turned swiftly. Rand had impressed him at the party, and here he was strolling along the avenue within grabbing distance. Irresistible!

"Hey, wait a minute!" shouted the Negro after Rand and churned madly through the massed strollers in the panic of a drowning man who thinks he has seen a straw float by him downstream; a straw, more-over, that is thwarting its *own* destiny by not mechan-ically presenting itself directly to him—for what straw was made but for a drowning man? So in a sense Hawkins felt that he was likewise coming to Rand's (or the straw's) rescue.

"Wait for me," he spluttered weakly, out of breath from the desperate swimming, and held onto Rand's arm.

"I'm afraid I don't . . . *oh yes,* at the Joneses'. How do you do?" said Rand, momentarily stunned. Man must be mad. And it seemed rather that he was holding Hawkins up, or pulling him to safety, to shore, than just shaking the man's hand in greeting.

"I caught you just in time," gasped Hawkins as they resumed walking.

"*Caught* me?"

Hawkins was still in the grip of confusion about the straw. *Caught* Rand just in time, meaning, it would seem, that in another moment Rand (the straw) might have in some way gone on to his destruction; but still there was that ambiguousness of *caught,* suggesting Hawkins' sense of being saved by the straw.

"You almost passed by," Hawkins more or less rationally explained.

"Oh, yes." What *is* he babbling about? Bad enough with my own dementia. On top of. . . .

"Do you remember Kirillov?" asked Hawkins, apparently quite recovered.

My God! Call the police? Just turn around and run for it? "Who?"

"You know, Kirillov. In *The Possessed*."

"Oh, *that* Kirillov. But what. . . ."

"I was just thinking of him when I saw you," Hawkins hastily lied. For in panic he felt that his simple unadulterated presence was not enough for acceptance, not quite, so he perforce had to make mad offerings, show that he was better than just a sordid human being like everybody else. "How unbelievably funny he was. Especially in his moment of supreme sacrifice, when he was bickering over trifles. Remember?"

It's so surreal I may as well take him for granted. No other way to assimiliate him. "Now that you mention it. . . ."

"Absolutely magnificent! Dickensian. And when he bit that chap's nose—what was his name?—just before shooting himself. Monumental humor! Really, I'm surprised that they haven't paid more attention to him."

They? "So am I," said Rand, pursuing his decision to comply with the man.

The Negro was silent for a moment, scanning the multitudinous forces so confidently floating by. Isn't good enough, he felt. Must do, say, something else, more tempting, more *personal.*

"Marzipan!" he suddenly blurted as a well-endowed young lady glided by them.

"Wasn't she though."

"That reminds me. I know where you can get some superb Harris tweed for almost nothing. In case you're in the market for a coat."

"Very kind of you."

"This chap I know brought in a lot of it from England and he can't use it all."

"I'll certainly keep it in mind," said Rand, still humoring Hawkins. "At the moment, though. . . ."

"I'll tell him to hold some for you then. He'll do this for me because he's such a close friend."

"Please, no." Too much, simply too weird for me at this time. Must escape. "Excuse me, but I have an urgent appointment. I'm hopping on this bus. Goodby," and he leaped into the welcoming mouth of a bus going in exactly the opposite direction from where he was actually bound.

"I'll call you!" the Negro shrieked after him. "I have tickets for *Swan Lake!*"

4

ᘐ

"LOOKS LIKE they're biting now," said
Harry as Eddie Brien.

"It sure does," observed Shanley, in a voice husky
with gratification and also further desire. "It sure
does. Won't be long now."

Their vigilant watch was being kept from a booth
on the other side of the one where the two girls, Edna
and Myra, were sitting alone, sipping beers. Eddie,
Shanley, and Mac, watching, waiting, poised there in
momentary restrained violence, like small hawks high
up, blood in their furious glazed eyes.

Harry was savoring the experience with both aspects
of himself, as Harry and as Eddie Brien; really in a
three-dimensional way, for besides the dual watch,
there was Harry watching Eddie, in somewhat the
same way a master, from a hidden window, might
observe his protégé down below in the yard, *living* it
out.

Yes, the two men at the bar who had been hotly glancing at Edna and Myra, indicating they did indeed wish to pick them up, now boldly left the bar itself and, balancing their drinks, more or less, strolled to the girls' booth and smilingly spoke to them, and then, the girls playing up to them, eased themselves into the booth.

"I hope they're from out of town," Shanley whispered.

"Why?"

"Two reasons: they'll be dumber and they'll have more dough."

"You're right, they will."

Mac began gently to crack his knuckles, but Shanley looked at him with such swift and concentrated distaste that he stopped, ashamed. Eddie was not at all afraid, and this pleased his mentor Harry. He sipped at the beer, but in the long waiting it had gone flat. Doesn't matter. He looked up at the bar and diverted himself for a few moments by staring at a middle-aged woman who was lushing old-fashioneds and mumbling to herself. A well-dressed Tugboat Annie. What Mesozoic lies was she comforting herself with?

"There they go," announced Shanley, soft joy in his voice.

"*Oh,*" murmured Mac, who was the youngest of the three.

The girls were sliding out of their booth (a quick signaling glance back at the three hawks) and the two men were helping them on with their coats, and the men appeared gay and pleased.

"Wait'll they leave the bar and turn the corner," advised Shanley.

"I have to hold myself back," Mac confessed anxiously, and Eddie smiled. Him too.

The moment the girls and the men turned the corner outside, Eddie and Shanley and Mac got away from their observation post and started after them. They were almost out of the bar when, "Wait a minute, wise guys!" was yelled at them.

Eddie's first instinct when he saw her was to smash her head in with a blow, for the fright she had thrown into them.

"I'm not giving no beers away tonight," the little waitress snapped, and held out her hand for it.

The three men looked at each other for an incredulous, relieved moment, then Eddie threw a dollar into the outstretched hand. They resumed their pursuit of the girls, not even bothering to wait for the little change they had coming nor the further remarks of the disturbed waitress. Eddie was a bit upset though. An omen? Loud-mouthed bitch!

They had to hurry from this point on. They caught

sight of the girls and the men halfway down the dark
side street, walking slowly, and laughing a little as
though somebody had just said something funny. The
river was nearby, and the strong, suggestive smell of
it clung to them now, urgently, seeming to activate
them.

"Look at them," breathed Shanley in contempt and
pleasure. "Think they've really got themselves a little
something, don't they?"

"To hell with them," snarled Mac.

"*There*," observed Eddie, as the girls, now at the
end of the dark street, abruptly turned into an alley.

In this alley Edna said to one of the men, "We'll
go in the back way."

"Anything you say, sweetheart," he replied. "But
what about a little one now?" and he quickly grabbed
Edna and kissed her, his drunk-clumsy hands fumb-
ling at her young buttocks and breasts.

She broke away from him. "Hey, take it easy, huh?
We're not there yet."

Myra and the other man watched this in some shyness. He had his arm around her, but mutely. He
broke his shyness and said, "You just can't wait, can
you, Hurley?" and giggled, as Myra did, only nervously.

"Come on, hon," ordered Edna, taking Myra's

hand. "We'll go in first, to make sure the coast is clear, and then you fellows come after us. O.K."

"Give us about a minute or two?" asked Edna.

She pulled Myra after her down into the dark stairway at the back of the building, and inside the building itself, leaving the two men alone in the dark alley, next to an open garage.

In seconds after the girls disappeared, one of the men, glancing momentarily toward the mouth of the alley, saw three figures enter it and come intently toward them. He was half drunk and this slowed his reaction to what he saw. But his instinct warned him more directly by spraying a sudden alertness into his body.

"What's this?" he begged of Hurley.

"Where?" And then Hurley saw too.

Seconds, and they did comprehend what it was all about, but they could not move from shock. At first, Hurley thought of his wife and home, how he wished he were there, and he was horribly frightened and wanted to whimper for mercy, like a little boy.

"Mess with my girl, will you?" cried Shanley appearing now directly in front of them in the darkness, and he hit Hurley in the face and knocked him down.

Eddie and Mac went to work similarly on the other man. They mercilessly beat both men unconscious, and in the fury of their assault they emotionally con-

vinced themselves that they really were saving the
honor of the two decoys, that it was not a simple trap
for unwary wolves, and this increased their assault,
gave it a manic moral imperiousness, justified it, puri-
fied it, if only for those few horrible seconds.

"Goddamn dirty lousy sons of bitches!" the boy
Mac whined as he hit Hurley again and again in the
face and stomach. He was almost out of his mind
with his terrible confusion.

Inevitably they finished their beating, and then they
dragged the unconscious victims into the garage and
robbed them of their wallets and watches. Eddie was
overcome by it, by the wonder of it, and the sheer
natural mechanics of the jungle. "It's the price," he
was saying to himself of the men and what had happened to them because of picking up the girls. "They
thought it was going to be a *handout! Unbelievable!*"

"Come on!" commanded Shanley. "We'd better
run for it. The girls are going to meet us down by the
bus station. Let's go."

And they fled down the dark river-moistened cobble-
stones, *away! away!*, loot in pocket, some slight blood
on hands, bodies behind them.

Doesn't know the difference between *belonging*
and *being*, reflected Rand. Can't he tell? or won't he
let himself think about it? But just what is he, what is

his *being?* Anything to a Negro being different from
other people? That's it, of course. I mean—can't he
be *that*, a Negro and a writer too, can't he see they
aren't mutually exclusive? Thinks you have to be a
white man if you want a brain. Stupid. And a *kind* of
white man. Now *that* is it, a *kind* of white man. Sissy,
he thinks, or distributor of endless gifts. Cuts his own
testicles off in process. Shame, a shame.

Feel like a son of a bitch running off like that, but
what could I. . . . *Swan Lake!* God! At this rate Hawkins would actually turn homosexual if he thought
that was *the way* to be. No self-respect, absolutely.
Makes him creepy. Dangerous. What finally does
identify one? *Oneself?* . . . . and not boogie-woogie
or yassuh boss either . . . something entirely different.
. . . He *is* different, that's the point! He *is!* Idiotic to
deny. . . . Really a sort of Madame Bovary. . . .

The bus debouched him from its yellowed belly,
gasping, shuddering, in hugest agony as it did, like
an elephant in labor, Rand thought, crossing the dangerous street and striding purposefully now toward
the vermilion asylum.

Then he was weaving in and out of the dreamily
drifting procession of green-clad figures and dark-
clad ones from outside, the landscape utterly changed
now, softer than back there, tender, almost breathing

and something in the atmosphere too, an amberness, an *underglow* perhaps, giving it an unreal dimension of mellowness, or *filtered, protected.* . . .

"But you aren't his family," the new nurse was saying to him at the desk. "You can't take him out. The rules are. . . ."

"I'm his closest friend, I'm closer than his family."

"What? *Closer?*"

"This is stupid. I've done this before, *before* you. It's understood. . . ."

"Dr. Graves, this gentleman claims—"

He did, however, get in and take Carter Barrows out, onto the green grass, despite a slight chill in the air.

"How did you hurt your hand?" he wanted to know.

Carter smiled and shook his head. "Defending my honor."

Like this, this is when I can't tell if he is or isn't. Weird two-headed statements like that. Watch myself. "Go on," Rand said.

"Woke up last night and a little boy from the other dormitory was trying to show me that all that matters in this awful world is love."

"Oh."

"Defending my honor, as I said. Have you ever defended your honor, Rand?" Carter asked shyly.

"Uh. . . ."

"I was just kidding. Forget it." He gazed calmly around the insane grounds, then returned. "They said I could go home for a weekend if I wanted. But I said no thanks."

Janine, Rand though immediately. She was afraid of this, of his coming home. Was I? But he *isn't*, not now. . . . "Why?"

"What's out there?" Carter continued. "At least they take care of you here," he looked at his bandaged hand, grinned, "except for a few things like this, of course. What would I do outside? Now anyway." .

Be a fool and try to tell him, make up some reasons why he should want to leave a crazyhouse for a couple of days and return to the other world. Go on, tell him.

"Nothing I can really say to that," Rand replied. "But what about . . . I mean, wouldn't you really like to be out . . . to see Janine differently, other people . . . just be out? I can't explain just what I mean." It's being here that does it, some dimension missing . . . equilibrium or references different. . . .

"How does Janine know I won't go batty again and saw off her breasts with a cake knife . . . or something like that? And how do *I* know?"

Carter paused, as if to rest from such a strenuous possibility, and plucked at cold grass blades. "Besides," he went on more softly, "I have a lot to think about before I see any of the people I used to know— other than you and Janine, of course." He paused once more, glanced at nearby trees. "She's very tough." When he looked back at Rand he had a vision of him and Janine lying in bed nakedly entwined, but at this moment it did not distress him. Later perhaps it would.

"I understand," Rand said. He's so lucid at times, too. Janine was worried about violence, but primarily just seeing him, especially now that she was doing something she thought she shouldn't. She was tough, but so fragile. So sweet. . . .

"Do you know, I've entirely lost my desire to drink since I've been in here," Carter announced.

"I'm very glad to hear that," Rand said. "You were drinking too much, a lot too much."

Carter stiffened at this. "What do you mean?" Attack.

Oh, he doesn't remember, that's the shock treatments. "Just that you drank much more than you had to, and it exhausted you, emotionally and physically."

"Were you thinking of any particular instances?" Carter inquired, staring tautly.

"No, of course not."

Afterward, after Rand had left, and he was sitting

on the lean, cold bed in his room, Carter thought
about what had gone on before. He picked up his notebook, and before making a new entry, glanced at the
old one. "Rand wants to destroy me, I know that. But
I will get to him first. He envies me."

Livingston strolled in, singing. "Do you recognize
that song?" he asked Carter gaily.

"Can't say that I do," replied Carter.

"I'll tell you why," Livingston said, "because it's
brand new. I just made it up." He smiled proudly.
"It's going to be on the Hit Parade soon."

"I'm proud to know you, Mr. Livingston," and
Carter took his loving hand.

"I'll be very rich," said the Negro.

"I hope you will, I honestly do."

Livingston lay down on his cot and began to sing
his new song again, while Carter began writing in his
journal:

"At this particular moment I feel that I could leave
here and go to another country without ever seeing
the people I know. There is nothing left there, nothing
at all. I could even begin a completely different
life. . . ."

On the other side of the room, Livingston, looking
straight up at the fathomless ceiling, as though he
were gazing into his own spacious nature, continued

to sing and invent his new song, his voice determined but quite gentle, and the tone bell-clear and sure. The song was all about love.

Margaret laughed to herself. "Like sleeping with an old tennis shoe!" she shouted to the room.

Phillips had just called and asked to borrow twenty dollars, and this unexpected request had set her off about him. Did I *really* like him at one time? she wondered. All this little-boy physical dirtiness . . . smart, yes, but . . . left her for a masochistic young schoolteacher . . . abandoned. So why do I even consider lending him this? Weakness, sloppy sentimentality . . . or *guilt?* For twenty dollars I can have Nina and Joey . . . certainly something for my money. It had been extraordinarily revivifying . . . most brilliant and effective . . . nothing remaining but sweet satisfaction, release, and hardly any dregs. . . . Dregs brought her back to Phillips . . . *they* gave me something for twenty dollars, but Phillips. . . .

Dressing now, she suddenly recalled a dinner party she had given when she was keeping company with Phillips. Not only had he eaten more of the food than anyone else, but after he had finished all his own he had actually asked Carter Barrows (who was drunk, and, incidentally, trying to feel her up under the

table) if he would give him a small gobble of the
steak on his plate. No shame, either, but boldly. And
oh . . . another incident . . . asking me if he could use
my apartment to entertain his brother and his wife
when actually it was to deflower a visiting debutante.
Inconceivable!

Standing before the mirror, she ran her hands feel-
ingly over her stomach and around her soft hips and
rump, measuring, but at the same time it was a ritual
she enjoyed physically, apart from its scientific end. . .
nice to feel herself . . . and she wondered if men did
the same thing. Maybe Phillips . . . yes, *he* would.

Later, after she had completed her morning appointment at the dressmaker's and, standing on the
avenue, was taking the measurements of the fearful
day, Harry bumped into her.

"Oh!" she gasped in real fear, for he had come
up behind her like a thief in the night and grabbed
her arm.

"What's the matter?"

"You frightened me for a moment." He had been
drinking, she could smell it on his breath. Gin. Maca-
bre sense of humor.

"That's one of the many normal incidents of life,"
he said.

"What's that?"

"Being frightened, of course. Nothing at all unusual about it. People seem to think it is though. Just
another aspect of their collective insanity."

Criminal, that's it, Margaret mused as they strolled
along. Something criminal about him . . . never seen
quite the same thing in anybody before . . . long lewd
nose. His poor wife . . . nice enough girl, though obviously not for him. What makes girls like her marry
such as he? Why do they hate themselves so much? "I
suppose you're right at that," she admitted.

"Whither bound?" he asked.

She told him nowhere in particular.

"I'll stand you to a drink then."

In the bar that he led her to, an unexpected turn
off the avenue, there were sailors and tired whores
and other nondescript riffraff, midday flotsam, dreaming long before nightfall, drawing about themselves
their own fabulous constellations, beered and whiskied
into celestial position.

Why here? she thought as they sat in a far booth.
What an *unlikely* place! If one were alone, up to something, cruising, that would be different; but with somebody one knows . . . the sour smell . . . the people . . .
they look as though they've been living inside a pulp
magazine all their lives. Is he being funny, doing this?

Think he's tough or something? Wasn't always that

way (assuming he's that now), no indeed. Quite the opposite when he was asked by that magazine to re- view a book of poetry written by a very good friend of his since departed for the Big Playground Upstairs. Afraid to do it, turned it down, because the friend happened to be under a vague cloud of political sus- picion, cloud since drifted by. And old fire-eater Harry thought any boost he might give the poor man would endanger his own position.

"Christ, Harry, this is *your own* loyalty test," they told him.

"It's too risky," he had whined, avoiding the eyes of the group as they sat around Phillips one night, and it wasn't a hundred years ago either. "Besides, I'm not so sure I like his stuff any more," and he had cringed.

He and Margaret drank whisky now and tried to look into each other.

"You scare me," he said.

She could hardly believe it, and from *him*. "*I* scare *you?*" she repeated in amazement, and she felt a prickly anxiety in her nipples.

He leered. "That's right."

"But how could I possibly. . . ."

"I'll tell you. You don't know what you're up to, you're fundamentally unmotivated. And anybody who lacks primary motivation is dangerous, you might say criminal. Do you follow me?"

What is this son of a bitch doing? Kinetic fear in
her now . . . *exposed*. Holding herself in, as a fugitive
would, crouched tensely in a doorway while his
hunters pant by, she said, "Not exactly, Harry."

He drank up, gazed over at the dreaming flotsam,
signaled the waiter for an encore, and went on.

"For instance, drinking from that jig's glass the
other night." Margaret winced. "Now what made
you do a thing like that? What point could it have?
What a peculiarly *vicious*—in the Aristotelian sense
—vicious gesture! How could you find identity in
such a thing?"

She could not, would not, reply immediately, for
she was too scared, and had to think of her ground.
So she just sipped the whisky.

"Don't you understand the necessity of *thinking*
about what you do?" he asked. "Once you begin to
think about it, you can do anything and it will have
meaning, but certainly not before."

The old waiter brought their fresh drinks and
Harry paid him—paid him, he now recalled, seeing
the crumpled currency (dirty but no bloodstains) with
his half of the trap-assault, with money from the two
vain suckers left unconscious in the river-scented alley.
This was funny . . . ironic. . . . Wonder if Margaret
would appreciate it? Could she afford to laugh at any
irony?

"Tell me, Lady M," Harry started, "who's your current amour?"

"I really don't see how that is any of your business, Harry."

"Now, now. You haven't by any chance got your roving optic on the classy Negro buck, have you?"

Margaret opened her mouth to speak, but at that very moment a voice inside the jukebox began to scream and moan hysterically, so loud it was shocking. It stopped Margaret, and it stunned Harry, for so supernatural was the timing, so prepared the dramatic moment, that for a crazy second it seemed to him that this was issuing from Margaret's mouth, and he stared, aghast.

"Oh!" Margaret gasped, now comprehending the horrible coincidence plus its supernatural *pertinence*, which made everything so utterly grotesque.

"Oh, I *hate* you!" she screamed, and in the same fluid motion threw her fresh highball into Harry's face, pushed free from the booth, and dashed frantically from that demented bar.

5

2

PHILLIPS WANTED TO MOVE, but he couldn't. He was paralyzed, but his mind was supercharged with aliveness. He lay there in mortal horror, waiting, unable to scream for help. Someone was slowly, powerfully pushing open his locked door, and Phillips knew that with the breakdown of the door would come his unbearably painful destruction. The person who was breaking in, he sensed, was a man, not a woman. Why *couldn't* he move, why *couldn't* he scream, why *him?* The pain and the fear, as he watched the door *now opening* in the dark, were so extreme that he wished for instant death, prayed to God for it. He opened his eyes. The scream stuck to roof of mouth.

"*What's the matter, darling?*" Freda whispered urgently, grabbing him, bringing him out into complete consciousness. "*What is it?*"

He sat up in bed and rubbed his hands over his face as if to restore the circulation of his being. "Someone was breaking. . . . Oh God," he muttered.

"Tell me what it is, darling. Please," she whispered tenderly, and pulled his shocked, thin-boned nakedness down to her tender, maternal warmth.

He lay there passively, enclosed and cushioned by her soft arms and legs and breasts, prenatally, and recovered himself from the nightmare. He had had three just like this since he had become Freda's young lover. She was pouring tenderness and warmth and almost audibly powerful waves of femaleness into him, and whispering sweet comfort to him. And he felt himself melting into forgetfulness and security. She put her comforting hand on his loins as though his fears, whatever they were, simple or complex, must inevitably come from there.

But suddenly something frightened him back to where he had been, and he disentangled himself and leaped out of bed.

"I've got to go home," he said sharply and began dressing in the darkness.

"But why?" Freda inquired in confusion and slight anger now. "What's the matter?"

"I can't explain it," he said, "but I do have to go, believe me."

She sighed heavily from the big bed, as though a child had just done something that was incredibly stupid yet quite natural and therefore futile to contest. "I don't understand you. You don't even try to be less mystifying ... peculiar. ..."

He was dressed. "Forgive me. I'll call you tomorrow. I'll try to explain it then." And hurriedly he let himself out of her apartment, her exasperated, inarticulate female groans and protests gently following him.

The fresh night air helped quite a bit, and although he lived fifteen blocks away, on the west side of the city, he decided to walk it rather than taxi there. He was sorry, but he had been *compelled* instinctively to leave that bed and that fathomless, insatiable body. He walked toward an all-night cafeteria, for coffee.

Once before ... he was tiredly trying to climb out of a swimming pool, by pulling himself up at the side. But he kept slipping back into the water, and gradually he thought he was going to drown in the pool. Suddenly Freda appeared, leaning naked over the side, to help him out of the threatening water. To pull himself out he was grasping her breasts, and was being helped out. But the milk began gushing from the breasts and he let go because it seemed he was being choked to death, and fell back into the pool.

Horrible, simply horrible, and he shook his head in
negation.

He chose a table in a far corner to drink his coffee,
a table with its back to the corner wall, a table viewing
all, assailable only from the front. Exotic night birds
twittered and fluttered at the shiny tables before him.
There was not one complete, bona fide, acceptable
member of the human race anywhere in sight.

What could be breaking through my . . . door?
What am I afraid of letting in? What beast is now un-
chained, wanting total freedom or recognition?

Recognize . . . could that be Carter Barrows over
there, sitting with that girl?—no of course not . . .
Barrows is still in the booby, thank God, for him and
for everybody else. What a jerk Carter had been!
Always bitching people . . . very feminine trait, despite his ostensible masculineness. The time he barged
into Freda's, drunk, blowing his stupid mouth off . . .
should have let him have it with the fire tongs. Rand
always going around apologizing for him . . . why?
Never understood that . . . peculiar friendship . . .
could see that he was totally incapable of *learning*,
letting himself see what was really going on in the
world . . . must have his private vision forced on to
the millions . . . manic delusions . . . quite natural
that the lid should come off . . . a wonder he didn't

vanish into thin air . . . *whoosh!* Maybe now he will
think a little about reality. Might help him in the long
run . . . but maybe not. Wonder what Janine will do.
To Rand? Too complicated. . . .

What am I doing thinking of *him!* Think of myself,
for God's sake! What's wrong? Screw loose? Running
out of a woman's bedroom in the middle of the night.

"The ant's a centaur in his dragon world . . . pull
down thy vanity, pull down". . . . That was it, if one
could be absolutely impersonal, outside (or above)
oneself . . . everything so much more workable . . .
wallowing in self-love . . . phew!. . . . no self-
respect. . . .

"The sugar?"

Big mottled Irish face, bloated dead hand on his
table.

"Go ahead. Take it."

"Lousy Jews that run this place won't even give you
enough coffee," the fat face blurted.

That was it! This filthy scum!

"You crummy bastard!" Phillips shouted standing
up. "I'm a Jew!" and without knowing exactly what
he was doing he smashed his fist into the mottled mass.

The man sat, or fell, into a chair and, stunned,
stared at Phillips but none of the lonely dodoes and
macaws at the other tables responded to the scene.

"Scum! Concentration-camp scum!" He was going to kick the man in his bloated face, as he would kick at a fanged antediluvian thing, rising up from the ooze with strange ideas in its slimy head, but he held back, raging, then walked rapidly from the cafeteria.

As he neared home, sobered, the insane fury quieted, he realized what an extraordinary gesture it had been. He had never done anything like that in his entire life, and he felt surprised and elated. As though in some complex way he had done penance, or had purged himself of, or even applied acid to, a pus-swollen wound.

"Nobody around paid us the slightest attention," he observed aloud to the sensitively listening night street, and shook his head in unbelief. Is that what it leads to, is that what one could become? And, almost to tease-torture, he saw himself with a mottled pig face, sugar bowl or truncheon menacingly clutched in a huge dead hand.

Upstairs in his apartment Phillips decided to think a little bit before resuming his dream life (he kept the night light on to thwart the cunning darkness). Why, he asked his entire generation out there, does anybody come to this cesspool of a city in the first place? Dirtiest spot in the country, certainly most vicious. Wouldn't trust my own mother here. Wouldn't trust *myself* here, which is more important. Everybody comes here to score. (The golden fleece. Ha!) Me too. Generation of scorers. And exactly *how* do I wish to score? First-rate question, and he knew the answer to it too, if he wanted to dredge it up and piece it together, but it made him twist too much, and he was sorry he had begun this midnight quest.

Stop shining that goddam light in my face! I'll confess! (Tomorrow.) Turn it off!

Whew! Hurry, sweet darkness, hurry.

The next morning he felt better. Over coffee he read his mail. Damn bills! Contaminated the other letters by their filthy presence. He strode to the bathroom and flushed them down the toilet in fierce aesthetic outrage. *Dreck!*

Good thing Margaret came through with that double sawbuck, or bid adieu to the lights and gas. She wasn't a bad sort, Margaret. A little neurotic, frigid—but all in all, as they say in Samarkand, within the pale. A little too afraid people are trying to take her. Must be characteristic of those to the manor born. Who is she going with now? Should have asked her. Why not? People too sensitive about such things, too private. Let's all sing like the birdies sing! Weird Anglo-Saxon sense of guilt, I suppose. They all see a burning stake in the distance . . . never really accepted the fact that they breathe . . . which is one thing I will say for the Jews, they have accepted that—what was that joke?—not only accepted it but could also probably learn to live under water. Ha! Those Jews, I love 'em . . . wouldn't dream of being anything else. Man would be crazy not to be one if he had the chance.

He had to go outside now into the detestible rain. Even for such a necessity as this it was hateful: he had to mail a letter asking for money. Why was money always connected with something unpleasant, physically distasteful? Very strange. (Another of those horrifying Anglo-Saxon equations, no doubt.) But this might be his masterstroke: a letter to a wealthy Middle-Western woman, known for her philanthropies, stating plainly that she should come to his aid, and in considerable quantity too.

He was, in effect, offering her the opportunity to become associated vitally with the artistic future of American culture, to wit, himself. Subsidize him in these lean years, be rewarded in the fat. (Biblical, after all.) And at the same time he would be a personal friend of hers—a voluntary, unnecessary gesture of his generosity—and as a companion do his level best to train her mind and sensibilities to a true

high-speed contemporary level. A bargain, looked at
from almost any *real* point of view, a downright bargain. Ten thousand dollars was a minimum for an
ordinary college education—and God only knows
what some well-known people had shelled out for what
they knew. Mrs. H. J. Parkinson of Blue Point, Michigan, registered letter, *par avion.*

Jobs, he'd had them, or they'd had him. And do you
want to know something, the real lowdown on jobs?
They stink! They're for ants, not human beings. Ruin-
ation of mankind. Messenger in a manufacturer's
office, counselor at a boys' camp, copy reader in a
publishing house—landed indirectly through Carter
Barrows. Just remembering them made him itch crum-
mily all over. Take me the rest of my life to cleanse
myself. The life of the mind, that's the ticket, me
bucko. But what about the old stomach and the thing
that keeps the wintry blasts off my poor head? He
remembered that when he had worked in the past,
before he rated full-time scrounging, his income had
taken care of these stupid items, and it had also made
him feel good, like a man, so to speak. But afterwards
he easily put the latter down as a bit of nonsensical
vanity, a tantalizingly stupid trap for the unwary. So it
no longer bothered him, that funny false pride. Would
he have to get another job? Positively, if this inspira-

tion didn't seven up. It *had* to! Baby needs new shoes!

"Every time it rains it rains pennies from heaven!"
Phillips sang hopefully, loudly, and strode bravely
out into the depraved downpour. "Hey nonny nonny
and a boop oop ee doop!"

Neither sleet nor rain nor gloom of night shall stay
this man from his self-appointed rounds.

The rain poured down on Janine too, as she waited
at the bus stop, streaking her face, staining her nyloned
legs, making her shrink into herself for warmth and
comfort. So sudden had the rain been that, in the context of the asylum back there, it seemed to her like
a malevolent inspiration from one of the inmates.
Trembled with cold and discomfort . . . feet getting
wetter and wetter . . . sudden rivulet down neck.

So the doctors thought he could come out soon, did
they?

"One of them wore a flashy yellow tie and looked
like a Broadway character," Carter had said, telling
of his examination by the board of psychiatrists. "And
I'm still not convinced he wasn't."

"He could still be a good doctor and wear vulgar
ties."

"I didn't say he couldn't. Only they certainly didn't
impress me, the way one feels scientists should im-

press one. It's funny how they can be specialists—intelligent and *right*—in one field and such mediocrities in most others. Isn't it?"

They were suddenly floating landscape figures when the rain sobbed down and they had to race across the greensward, with those other humbled figures, to steamy safety inside.

"Isn't that strange?" Carter yelled as they ran.

"I don't know!" Janine had yelled back, almost slipping to her knees on a soft spot of mud.

The bus arrived, exhaust stinking, and she climbed into its crowded sanctuary. She resumed thinking of her visit to the asylum.

"Wanted to know why I thought anybody would wish to railroad me into this place," he had said.

"Yes?"

"Told them that I didn't think that any more," said Carter, now they were safe inside the visitors' lounge.

"That's certainly a good sign."

He had examined her most closely then, trying to detect what?

"At the same time, I don't know what to think. Very confusing. Damn shock treatments . . . my poor brain will never be the same."

"They say it does go back to normal after a while," she volunteered.

"Assuming that's where you want it to go back to."
He paused to look about at his fellow prisoners and
their whispering, humiliated visitors. They act just
like they're in an art gallery, he mused. Stop your
goddam whispering! he wanted to shout. "Anyway,
they put me through the hoops, and I was very cagey,
stayed away from the moon, and they said I was
almost ready for good-by. Asked me about my plans
for the future."

On the bus, she inched down the aisle a little because the man crowded directly behind her was indulging his proximity to her a bit too self-consciously.
Pig!

"What *are* your plans for the future?" she had
fearfully asked Carter.

He laughed and rolled his eyes in mock fiendish-
ness. "Next installment, my dear. Doors open at
noon."

Exasperating! "But I'm your wife. Don't be so
funny please."

He became serious and looked at his folded hands.
"I really haven't any plans."

Sudden guilt in her. "Of course, there isn't any
hurry. No rush. I only meant. . . ."

But he was not listening, he was looking at his
hands, and drifting far, far away into himself. She

waited for him to return. The tormented faces were all around her, but she did not let herself think about them. She suddenly saw and then concentrated upon an isolated white hair in Carter's sideburn, sticking straight out like a spear she might have flung.

He looked up in a few seconds and said, "The yellow-tie man asked me if our sex relations had been good." He laughed. "What a bunch of voyeurs!"

"How is the boy who jumped from the window?" asked Janine. Anything to get him off this tack.

He penetrated her. "How did you know about him? I didn't tell you about him."

_What made me say it! "Rand told me about it. He was here when it happened, wasn't he?"

Still staring at her. "*He* told you . . . what other little things does he tell you?"

What will I do when he gets out? What am I supposed to do with him? Do they think about that? Do they think they're giving me a great big Christmas present?

Rand was already there when she arrived, in her apartment using the secret key (that had been Carter's), a warming drink in his hand. He looked almost but not quite natural there. He's been so wonderful and close during this entire horrible mess and I'm so stupid I don't even know why. Is it for *me?* Please let it be.

"It's a miserable," she said, throwing off her wet coat, "it's miserable . . . *outside,*" and suddenly she began to sob uncontrollably, and Rand drew her to him on the sofa. Great shaking, wracking sobs, soul sobs, awful.

Some time later, after they had risen, become then lovers, Janine said she would most certainly have to tell Carter, but of course this could not be done until he had been discharged, quite cured, was in strong condition and could absorb it without too much shock, which might send him back to where he'd pulled himself up out of.

Rand, however, though now a lover, was neither yet so committed nor courageous; but there was no manly way for this to be said, or even indicated, so he did not say please wait, no fatal thrust just now—and his silence of course meant agreement. He did not even know yet what *did* keep driving him to see Carter as regularly as if he were his father confessor or special doctor. *Why?* I don't like the guy *that* much.

"We must not let anyone know," he said.

"Of course," she replied. "Of course," for now the fact of guilt was there, no longer fantasy.

"People simply love to talk," Rand said. "This

would bring out all their free-floating malice," in partial explanation, so as not to seem cowardly, also as though it were *reputation* that mattered.

He made them both a drink while she prepared dinner (for the first time since Carter's departure).

"I've decided to go to the ballet with Hawkins after all," he told her, while she prepared the raw meat.

"But why? Don't you detest the ballet?"

"Yes, but he thinks it's him I detest, not it, if I turn him down. He's called me three times."

"But doesn't he have any friends? I mean, anyone like himself?"

"The point is," Rand continued, indirectly, "I don't know precisely what he wants, what he's after. But I'm positive it isn't me, and that makes it very subtly humiliating, in a way I'm sure he doesn't understand."

Searing of raw flesh, sudden hot fragrance of it in the room.

"Rare, or medium?"

"Rare."

Flesh burning at stake, it occurred to him in that scented moment. Yes, but whose? *Whose?* And when, minutes later, the warm blood spurted in front of him, he was still asking: But whose? *Whose?*

Edna pirouetted gaily. "You like it, huh?"

"Sensational," Harry said. "It's sensational, no kidding."

"O.K. then. I'll keep it, if you like it."

Her new skirt was black velvet and she had just bought it with her share of the money from the cobbled alley. They were in the roominghouse where Edna and Myra lived together. Smelled of girls' clothes. . . . and something else, secret and intimate.

"Should I wear it now?" she asked him.

Knowing how perverse it might sound, Harry replied, "Why do you ask me?"

Edna looked puzzled at first, then she slowly smiled and said, "Because I like to have you tell me to do things, that's why."

Lovely, just lovely. Precisely what I was hoping she would say.

"It makes me feel funny and good, like the shivers," Edna went on, standing in front of his chair.

He bent forward and playfully slapped her on the buttocks. "It does, does it?"

The last time he had done this, made this gesture, had been with his wife. She had disliked it and remarked that it was vulgar. At this moment, he reflected, she was probably marking term papers. Edna, thank God, was a waitress, to say absolutely nothing in the difference of *elan vital* . . . no comparison at all.

"Eddie, did you know that Shanley had a gun?" she asked him later as they were walking to the restaurant to pick up Myra, who also worked with Edna.

No. Front page of the *Daily News* appeared in his mind first—policemen standing around—and after that came, "He's a smart guy, he knows how to lay his hands on a lot of things besides girls. But how did you know?"

She was holding onto his arm. "He showed it to Myra last night."

A *gun*—unexpected, new, even alarming to him on one level of his complex self, but then on another most exciting and imaginative. Eddie in him was already handling the gun, taking it into his life, while Harry in him said, I've never shot a gun. Don't they backfire or kick back? No, *recoil*, that's the word, *recoil*. Tonight he was wearing a black shirt with collar buttoned (but no tie) because Eddie felt this style made him appear at once attractive and complicated.

"What'd he say about it?"

"He was going to talk to you about it tonight. Which reminds me," she added, "what are we going to do tonight?"

"I don't know, something or other."

"It'd better be good."

"It will be," he promised her, and he caressed the small of her back. She had already given him a snapshot of herself, which he had, while she watched, put in the special wallet he carried as Eddie Brien. Pleased her.

That crazy bitch Margaret . . . throwing that drink in his face! However, after he had recovered he had laughed screamingly, it struck him as so ludicrous. But must not think of any of that back there . . . and he pushed it out of thought and bore down intensely to revive Eddie Brien.

"It's a beaut, Shanley," Harry was telling his friend. They—he and Edna, Shanley and Myra, and Mac—had just come away from the bowling alleys and were standing in a dark spot next to a parked car. He gave the gun back to Shanley.

"You ain't even asked me where I got it," Shanley observed with a proudness.

"O.K."

"Found it in a parked car!"

"Found it!" Mac snorted with pleasure.

The girls admired it too, but fear and awe were in their voices when they murmured, and they handled it most delicately, as though it were a powerful symbol that had lain buried for thousands of years and must be properly propitiated, or else its magic would go wrong. Suddenly Edna plucked it from Shanley's hand. She stared at its hard beauty, gently stroked its smooth barrel, and then, closing her eyes, kissed it, as the others watched in silent amazement.

Something in Harry swooned at that passionate gesture, swooned in deepest thrill.

"What'd you do *that* for?" Shanley demanded, now recovered from his awe.

"Yeah, what for?"

"*Edna,*" whispered Myra.

Edna was embarrassed. "I don't know," she said. "I just had to do it. So forget it, will you? Just forget it."

But they had all been strongly affected by it, despite their surface show of cheap incomprehension (even Edna's *near* denial of her own worshipful act), and they walked away in mood of religious revelation. Harry took Edna's arm this time.

Beer in Hanlon's Bar. I have not felt so *alive*, real, since I was ten years old, Harry mused, but he was speaking for Harry and not Eddie, for the latter was totally there, was not observing but was actually *it*. (Such confirmation for Harry!) His Eddie belched very loudly, in exaggeration, and they all liked it.

Though Shanley was joking and fooling with Myra, he was still restless. They had a gun, and this too was life that could not be denied or suppressed like some primitive desire, say, to spit on someone's shoe. No, not at all, too strong, too urgent a presence, too full of passion. (Edna's hand was on his leg under the table.)

"You didn't miss anything today," Myra said to Edna.

"No?"

Myra shook her head. "Lousy. I made exactly two-twenty in tips. How do you like that? The place was like an iceberg."

"Cheapskates go there anyway," observed Mac. He knew the restaurant well, it seemed.

I don't like him, thought Edna. Why is he always alone? Pimples too, too old for it . . . couldn't stand to touch them, make me sick. "You said it," she agreed. What made me crazy, kiss that gun that way? Something must have come over me. Jesus! But I *did* like it and I wanted to. . . .

Harry bought them all a round of beer.

"My hand hurts from that guy the other night," he said.

Shanley laughed. "Was worth it though, wasn't it? I bet you get your hand hurt dipping them pictures

when you work, too, but you don't get paid like that
for it."

"You're a real businessman, Shanley." ⸺

"You have to be."

Myra smiled at this. "When are we going to do it
again. It was fun, huh, Edna?"

"Uh huh. It scared me but I liked it."

Now the gun's presence was felt. "I know what,"
Harry spoke up, almost involuntarily, as though he
were just a medium for the group, or even for an
abstract situation. This was Eddie. "What about the
bowling alley? Do you remember the guy at the booth
there?"

Shanley breathed respectfully. "Oh yeah. You hit
it, Eddie, you really hit it this time."

The two girls quickly exchanged fearful but conspiratorial glances, cueing each other's emotions.

"But where do we come in?" asked Myra.

"Lookouts," Harry explained simply.

Mac clapped Harry on his drape-suited shoulder.
"Boy, you're getting the spirit!" He turned to Shanley.
"Didn't I tell you this guy was okay? Didn't I?"

And Edna's young hand was squeezing its admir-
ation under the table. She believed in him, absolutely.

6

℮

HAWKINS' FATHER stands over him, huge and black, and thunders, "Remember this, boy! You better be yourself in this life, 'cause it's sure you can't be nobody else!"

I absolutely agrees with you, Poppa! But *how? Please* tell me how!

That had been long ago, of course, in one's lost boyhood, but Hawkins still did remember it and it still frightened and confused him. How does one be oneself? Who was he, so that he could be him? He was still shipped out on that desperate voyage, but he so wished that it were over, quite settled. He glanced up at the woman on the wall who had been looking down on him this unexpected afternoon. Made her bundle slave-trading, no doubt, and here I am squatting in her granddaughter's hold wishing she would ask me to be hers! "Please, Hawkins, be a good chap, and

marry me, will you? Save me from myself." Even if
she did it only for laughs, even then I'd accept it,
want it.

"Forgive me for intruding in your dream life, Mr.
Hawkins, but would you care for some fresh Scotch?"

"Oh!" he said, startled back. "I'm sorry. Yes,
please," and he smiled gratefully at Margaret for her
hospitality. "Love another one." She was getting
drunk, obviously, but why? for what special reason?
me? And the other one, the Johns woman, she's not
exactly stone cold herself.

"And then you went to Oxford," Roberta Johns reminded him.

"Oh, yes!" he almost shouted, picking up the thread
again. "Then I went to Oxford and got my degree in
Elizabethan literature. Returned to this country and
was fortunate enough to get a fellowship which has
enabled me to continue my studies."

Of course, Margaret was thinking, that explains the
accent, but not *why*, though. Bestial-*looking* . . . depraved combination, that face, that voice . . . get him
drunk and then see what exotic fauna rear their pretty
heads. . . .

Roberta Johns smiled very sweetly across the room
at him. "Herrick's my favorite poet."

How incredibly generous the dirty bitch thinks she's being! *Herrick!* Johnny Walker more likely.

"Get up, get up for shame!" he suddenly shouted.

There he goes, Margaret observed, I thought so.

Stunned looks first; then, Roberta said, "Of course, 'Corinna'!"

". . . 'The blooming morn upon her wings presents the god unshorn'—Yes," Hawkins sighed, spent now, "He's one of my favorites too." I must be going crazy.

"Beautiful," Roberta said devotionally. He's more attractive than I first thought. Invite him to another party. Could be shaped. Must go now. Margaret's getting restless. I can tell, wants me to leave, to leave her with him. Beautiful girl, charming, but. . . . And she drank up. Phillips and Harry and his wife were to be at her place for dinner.

"You should make poetry readings. Have you ever thought of it?" Margaret asked him some time after Roberta had gone, and Hawkins, at her insistence, was on his fifth Scotch highball. They had already exhausted Roberta as subject matter.

"Yes," he lied. Why not? he thought. What difference does it make? All this is just phony communion anyway. No, missy, I never thought of making poetry readings, but I used to stand for hours before my Cambridge mirror reciting Chaucer in Middle English, and once I cried because that was not *my* language, and once I almost asked the Players if I could be Othello, it would have been the finest since Ira Aldridge, but I lost my nerve, and yes, wept again on that occasion. Wouldn't she love to hear that! Top-drawer stuff all right. He drank the rest of his high-ball in one gulp. I *am* drunk now, and he stroked his beard in self-love and intoxication.

"Well, I have a friend who owns a small jazz-recording company," Margaret said, "and I'm sure that if you called him, something could be worked out." She felt drunk enough now to do what she wanted, and she started walking across the room toward Hawkins, standing at the Capehart examining her record collection.

"That's awfully kind of you," Hawkins said, turning to see her approaching him. "I'm most grateful to you."

She stood in front of him, and he very quickly saw how far gone she was.

"Would you excuse me if I do something bad?" she asked, thick-voiced.

"Why, yes," he replied automatically, and his breath held back.

"I want . . ." she began; and while he watched her,

stunned, she began to unbutton his shirt for the taste
of his dark forbidden skin beneath.

Rand looked at his watch again, impatiently. Damn
him! He's half an hour late, and after he went to all
that trouble to get me down here too. Then he thought
of something: Maybe he's done it on purpose, maybe
he's standing me up to show his independence and
contempt for the whole silly business. Rand snorted.
Ha! That would be something. Damn well serve me
right too. I would really take off my hat to him. I hope
that's it, I honest to God do.

The in-going crowd swirled around him, buffeting,
gabbling, and now Rand was caught up in it. He decided, now that he was here and had waited so long,
that it would be stupid not to go in anyway. He therefore bought himself a single ticket and was shortly
thereafter witness to the frenzied spectacle inside.
What an inspiration, if that's what he's done!

A firebird winged onto the stage.

Before Hawkins opened his bleared eyes, his body,
working faster than his fogged mind, thought it was in
the wallowing hold of a ship. Sea-wracked, salt-sick.
. . . Then his eyes did open and he saw Margaret lying
white-naked next to him, asleep, or out cold. Hawkins

had been seduced by white women before but never in quite such a fashion as this. He shuddered faintly as it all began to come back to him. No, time enough for recollection later on. Nicer to think of the last occasion: a wrenlike woman, lesser English nobility, had thought it was her duty to redeem him (more or less regularly, in an unused maid's room), as though he were some sort of delinquent child. *Please, Lord, purify this poor man with my orgasmic bliss.* A bit of all right, too. And afterward, in Gothic-terraced comfort, they munched paté sandwiches and sipped tea and discussed British socialism.

His eyes hurt. I shouldn't have let her pour all that dreadful stuff down me. He continued to gaze at Margaret's brilliantly naked body as he tried to collect himself. Wonderful heavy legs, rich, and he could not resist bending down and tenderly kissing her thigh, just below the karakul. Then something robotlike in Hawkins pulled him off the bed to dress himself.

He weakly reached the floor for his skin-tight suit of long woollen underwear. (His skin, beneath the unbuttoned shirt, had not been black after all, Margaret had seen.) If he had even dreamed this was going to happen this afternoon he would not have worn them, but her sudden call had quite confused him. He had been in Paris, the previous winter, where the cold had

been so cruel, so Gallicly heartless, he thought surely
he was going to die. Of all such things Hawkins could
not bear the cold; it depressed him, it confused him,
it frightened him. Now wasn't there something. . . .

Oh my God! as he remembered.

The ballet! Rand. . . . God help me!

And seized with an almost unbearable anguish and
anxiety, Hawkins threw a coat over himself and raced
from Margaret's apartment. Thank heaven the Opera
House was just two blocks away, he figured in the
rational part of his mind, but in the other part, the
frightened, fetid swamp of childhood terror, he saw
his whole future being wrecked through this gross
stupidity—Rand would never speak to him again, then
he would tell Harry and the others, and they in turn
would. . . . "Oh forgive me!" he moaned aloud as
he sprinted through the amazed streets. "Forgive me!"

In *Swan Lake* there is a moment when the stage
becomes still as the breathless female dancers (now
pure white swans), await the dreaded manly archer
who, crossbow in hand, suddenly leaps onstage with
murder in his heart, at which instant the orchestra
rages in with full dramatic fury.

In this exquisitely suspended pause, this most fragile hiatus, the audience was suddenly distracted by
strange wild cries coming from the back of the theater.
Then, just as on the stage the archer made his great

spring, they saw a bearded Negro sprinting down the long aisle pursued by two ushers. One usher grabbed at the demonic figure, but pulled only his black cape off, and the Negro leaped free, looking, in his white skin-tight suit, like one of the dancers, and then as he leaped high and wildly from the grabbing hands the orchestra roared in, and it seemed to the audience, for a stricken second, that this was a maniacal addition to the ballet itself.

"Catch him! He broke in!" the ushers howled against the orchestra's fury.

"I'm late! I'm sorry! I'm late!" Hawkins screamed to Rand huddled in his seat. Rand, his sense of reality already enervated by the fantasies on stage, thought he must be having a vision.

"You're wrong, that isn't what I meant at all," said Harry, shaking his head.

Roberta Johns sighed. "Then what *did* you mean?"

"Simply this: the American upper middle class isn't *being* destroyed, it's destroying *itself*. And do you want to know why? Because it refuses to experience anything."

Across the room Phillips waited intently for Harry to proceed. He frequently paid homage to Harry's mind, but just as often he did not know whether to take him seriously. He was—or at least had been in

days past—so contradictory that Phillips, in some disappointment, had regarded him as a gifted clown, not
too much more. But there it went again—the eternal
need to judge! To be absolute, black or white. Very
bad, stupid. Still, what about the time when Harry
forsook him? Or rather, times. Hadn't Barrows drunkenly bitched him, Phillips, all one evening when he
wasn't there to protect himself?—but Harry was there,
and according to his informant had not said one word
in his defense. Unforgivable, Phillips thought now,
unchristian. And didn't he back down when he was
asked to recommend Phillips for the job at the Foundation (which he got anyway), explaining subtly that
he never recommended anybody for anything because
it set up a bad situation!

"I'm afraid I don't—" began Roberta, glancing,
as if for help, toward the others—Phillips, Harry's
wife, her own husband.

Harry leaned forward aggressively.

"You can only exist in so far as you function, function spontaneously, organically. In other words, *react*.
All right. The upper middle class in this country
doesn't do these things. By now they live so exclu-
sively by formula, and by preconceived patterns, that
they are in effect merely somnambulists, or robots, or,
as I said, corpses. Even their speech," here he smiled
from a sense of sheer futility, "even their speech has

become pure gibberish. It's an argot of completely esoteric, arbitrary symbols, clichés, and vocal nuances, utterly removed from contemporary reality."

Roberta's husband laughed, but it was rather more of a relieved, irrelevant laugh than a direct response to what he had just heard, and it did almost visibly relax the concentration that had been built up in the room. "You sound as though this pleases you, Harry old boy," Johns said amiably.

"As a matter of fact it does," replied Harry. "Any contribution I can make to the process of their extinction, I will make gladly. We've had them with us far too long." And he leaned back in his chair as if actually waiting to view the imminent physical sight of this quite, quite delightful phenomenon.

"Christ, Harry," remarked Phillips, "you sound a little the way Carter Barrows used to."

"No. The trouble with Carter was that he wanted to destroy a whole generation," replied Harry.

"That's nothing," Phillips returned. "You want to destroy the whole of Western civilization!"

Harry threw up his hands in mock despair. "At least I'm not motivated by personal vanity. Carter just wanted to wipe out his contemporaries. How vain!"

"Oh Harry—*really*," his wife said, indicating the limit of her endurance.

Really? She doesn't even know the meaning of the

word—nobody here does. Really is from real, and who here is that? There but for the grace of time and space and several million other things sits Edna. Would that it were. Have never seen any single act so passionate, so felt, as her kissing that pistol. Christ, it was just like having her. . . . And she used it too! They had returned to the bowling alley just before its closing hours, somewhat beered up, and from a back window saw that all was prime. The manager was counting out the day's receipts, and only one lone bowler remained on the long garish alleys. The girls were told to stand outside, by the entrance, to keep watch. If anyone came in they were to make a signal, warning the men inside. It was agreed that Harry was to use the pistol. Because he had. . . .

"No!" Edna cried, just as they three stepped inside. "No!"

The three men stood still, looking at her.

"I want to," she said, stepping forward.

"You?" Shanley said, dumfounded, reflecting Harry's reactions as well.

"Yes. I want to use it," and it was then apparent to them that the same irrational, or inspired, feeling that earlier had put her lips to that cold steel, was now urging this.

The three looked at one another, and Myra too,

shrugged; then, somehow quite naturally Mac stepped to Myra's side, taking Edna's place, and from inside his plastic-belted pants Shanley handed her the pistol, and she and Harry and Shanley walked inside. For that urge in her could obviously not be denied.

And she had not faltered either. Cool and authoritative, on top of it every second. . . . must have been that way with Jeanne d'Arc . . . an instrument of fanatical passion.

Shanley scooped away the money from in front of the dazed manager (bald-headed with glasses), Edna holding the gun, while Harry bullied the lone bowler. It was very quickly over, a stroke swiftly dealt. Telephone ripped out. But just as they were leaving, or turning away toward going, the manager came out of his ice of fear and swung at Edna.

"Gimme that . . ." he yelled as he swung.

And Edna jumped out of his desperate reach and shot him. Blood came out all over his shoulder and in awe the man put his hand to it. Then it had to be done. Shanley tore the gun away from Edna and felled the bleeding man with a blow to his head.

"Bastard!" Harry said of the fallen man, and they ran out. (The lone bowler was left caged in the lockable women's lavatory.)

Outside, they joined Mac and Myra, and calmly,

exactly like ordinary citizens, walked to the corner and hailed a cab.

"Was there much?" Myra asked excitedly.

Then Edna was utterly changed, returned to what she had been, consummated, tranquil. Harry pulsed hotly with pleasure, pure animal brutality but essentially, he thought in the getaway taxi, *alive*, existing, no cliché here, no formula, no vacuum symbol, absolute original communion. And then Eddie Brien saw the money, felt the quick power, the sheer whistling surface velocity of it and wanted to be where he could uninhibitedly swagger. Not bad, not bad at all, this person was saying to himself, and the streets flew by like cast-off years of his life.

"Why did you shoot?" the boy Mac asked Shanley.

"Yes, I agree with you, Harry," Phillips was remarking. "There must be an absolutely new start, a total reformation. Perhaps nothing short of demolishing Western civilization, as you more or less suggested a while back. Because it's sure that something awful has gone wrong, a fantastic falseness or basic misunderstanding."

"Another deluge . . . forty days, forty nights."

"I mean it," Phillips protested to the Johns woman, who thought she was being funny.

"Change white to black, black to white, wrong to

right, taste to vulgarity, intelligence to stupidity—
there's a beginning," suggested Harry, and leaned toward Mr. Johns to mutely beg a cigarette, finger to
mouth. He glanced too at his wife, but she really
wasn't listening. She thought she had heard it all before, and besides, what did it matter?

"And then what would happen?" blond Mr. Johns
inquired of Harry.

Harry looked at him quite seriously. "Do you really
want to know?"

Handsome groomed face smiled. "Sure."

"All right, I'll tell you. If all existing standards of
behavior and morality were abolished, it might then
be possible for modern man to live within the full, rich
complexities of his possibilities. Without which he is
a destroyed dream."

Compared to him, mused Phillips, I'm not even in
my novitiate. Funny that it should be going on in the
home of the very people who would be the first to go.
Voyeurs, parasites, well-groomed barnacles. If you
don't like it, of course, you can leave. No gun in your
ribs.

"Don't pity the poor Russians, pity yourselves," he
said. "Right?"

"Absolutely," Harry joined, nodding his head em-
phatically at Phillips.

"Anarchy!" Johns exploded.

"No, not anarchy; *faith*." And Harry again leaned back in that huge chair to observe the panorama before him. The smoked poured from his nostrils. His wife left the room for something, and Harry wished she would fall out a window. Or simply put on her coat and abandon him. No, that would be asking too much.

Too bad Mr. Hawkins isn't here this evening, Roberta reflected. Where is he? I wonder if he spends much time with other Negroes, or are his affections all blanched white? And she got up to place a dish of toasted almonds on the cocktail table, salt-free, within Phillips' arm's length. *Her* contribution.

"You're so peculiar," Johns suggested, again in his half-smiling way, to Harry.

"How?"

"Well, your ideas, your. . . ."

Harry shouted: "I'll tell you the fundamental difference between me and most people. While everybody else is striving to give their existence *purpose*, I, on the contrary," and he rose up in his chair, "am striving to give purpose *existence!*"

The Negro guard at the locked steel door to Ward B slowly unlocked the door and allowed Carter to pass through.

Children and the insane are entrusted to them,
Carter thought. Why? Must be some very special
reason . . . nothing to do with economics either. Dark
hands I love to touch me. Magic, of course, plain and
simple magic. Place is full of magicians, all sorts.
The way they watch you too—use their eyes like no
white man has used his in a thousand years. Always
watching me, though. They're getting in a rut.

"Ah! Monsieur Groz! What brings you here to our
humble abode?"

"There's something I would like to discuss with
you," Groz announced, coming to within a few inches
of Carter's face.

His breath smells like a cat's. Wonder what Jesus'
smelled like.

"Why me?"

"Because. Let's go into that corner, where we can
be alone."

Instinctively, Carter glanced around to see if they
were being watched. The two white-suited Negro
guards were lounging in boredom at the door, not
caring about at all about the inmates. And, at this
moment, none of the other green-clad men were peer-
ing suspiciously about.

"Okay, let's go."

A moment ago he had not felt like this at all, not

at all conspiratorial or pursued. It was Groz's influence.

In the far, safe corner, Groz quickly slipped a letter inside Carter's jacket.

"Please mail this!" he whispered urgently. "Give it to your wife."

"But what is it?"

"I'm asking a doctor I used to know to get me out of here. They can't keep me here against my will, when I'm as sane as any of them."

"Why can't you mail it, though?"

"Because they open all my letters. *I'm a prisoner here*, don't you understand?"

Yes, he did understand. Carter had been—still was —a prisoner, against his will. Victim of a subtle conspiracy, formed, he sometimes was sure, by the closest of his friends. But then this wasn't quite so, he knew. Still, something strange. . . . They told him he could leave soon, though. A trap? A lie? Certainly find out damn soon.

"All right, Groz," he said, agreeing in the desperate errand.

Groz swiftly grabbed his hand and kissed it.

"Stop it!" Carter hissed, and wiped the moist spot of gratitude off on his tight green prisoner pants.

"But you're so kind, I had to do it," Groz whimpered, poised for sudden tears.

Kind! I had to go insane to hear that word linked to my poor name. The city used to fairly ripple with stories of what an impossible person I was. People babbling constantly. The city and he, he recalled, had almost always been at odds, one trying unceasingly to elude and deceive the other. All night long he could hear the faint noise of thousands of secret burrows being dug underground. It was almost all he could do to keep track of them.

They thought they were so smart, so brilliantly cagey, but he had soon enough let them know that he was on to them, and more. Infrequently, though, in uncharacteristic lapses of his guard, it had occurred to him what a preposterous business it all was. How in the name of Christ had the whole thing been set up, or rather agreed to? for there had to be some sort of agreement (like corruption or murder it did take two). What had driven him to such a maze? Why hadn't he stayed put? Suicide pattern? But if that were true, then the city was populated almost entirely by potential lemmings. Of course history is full of groups, and cultures, bent on self-destruction, building cliffs so they can throw themselves off them.

Had lost his nerve after a while, and had frantically tried to hide this awful fact. The most shameful thing of all, he had thought, losing nerve. He remembered now discussing it with one of the doctors there. The doctor had managed somehow to touch on *the very nerve*, and Carter had broken down in sobs. Coward, coward, coward. Dirty yellow coward, stupid yellow coward. Why, why, he sobbed, couldn't they just let him live—or why couldn't he let himself—like the ignominious filth he was? And after that avalanche it had been quite nice to contemplate a whole new existence (like suspended animation). Why is it so much better to win than to lose? What's so great about a hero? It's so easy, any fool can be a hero, but who can be a coward, and a loser? Me! Waves and waves of new pleasure had flowed around him. *There is nothing wrong with it. Forgive yourself before it's too late.*

Groz's saucer eyes were brimming, one still mauve from the hard fist of a sympathetic, cooperative inmate.

"What are you waiting for?" Carter asked him. "I agreed."

Then, not staying for Groz's confused answer, he walked away.

"They're going to give Groz insulin," Bone had said yesterday. "Find out why he *don't* tick."

Rand had come today; had, in fact, by the hospital rules, just a little while ago personally delivered him to that implacable steel door and that large dark magician lounging there now with a comic book in his grasp.

He had meant to ask Rand—very cleverly, of course —if he had told Janine about the man who had leaped through the window. Trap him. But they had been sidetracked by other things, unfortunately. But there will be time, time to murder, time to create. . . .

"It involves the whole question of health—what health is," Rand had said.

"Tell me, what is it?"

"I'd sound like a fool if I did, Carter."

"Go ahead. I won't betray you if you do."

Rand had smiled at that.

"Well, I'm really not sure what it is. But I do know that it can't be any arbitrary, rigidly conceived thing; it has to be elastic and relative to be at all acceptable." He paused to collect the evasive fragments. "In fact, I'm not sure the very concept of health, as we know it, isn't naïve, or at least uncontemporary in the broadest sense."

He wouldn't be talking to me like this unless he thought I could take it, Carter had reasoned. Except if he's attacking me, undermining. He has it in him, everybody has, but I doubt it from him. On the other hand, sometimes Rand, on these visits, seemed to be talking partly to himself. Difficult to put one's finger on it.

"What's *your* idea of a healthy person?" he asked.

Rand glanced quickly at him, momentarily suspecting some kind of sly paranoid trickery. But saw none. "Like choosing Miss America," he said almost shyly.

"I'd seriously like to know, Rand."

Rand thought it over a minute before answering. "You," he said finally.

If he is often really talking to himself when here, does this mean he thinks he is a healthy person? Surely not *me*.

"That's not funny."

"And I'm not a comic," Rand said. "Here: at least you put up a fight—that's a sign of it. Most people just accept all of the big lie out there, outwardly and inwardly, so there's no quarrel. The man who breaks down does so because he won't accept it all, finds it a fraud, even when it's in himself and not just out there. The world is full of adjusted robots, millions of them. Do you see? And now, having done it, you have a chance that we don't have. You've seen yourself as few people do. That's almost luck. You've had the complete experience of self."

There it was: that strange double level of meaning he always got from Rand, as though he operated in two dimensions, not the usual one. That's what makes it seem at times that he is me. Kind of psychic double-jointedness. But he was right about the experience of self, though I'm not so sure about his health talk.

"The great challenge, or responsibility, is to live up to it, not try to tell yourself it didn't happen," Rand continued.

"Did you hear me?"

It was Bone talking to him now.

"No, what did you say, Bone?"

"I said they're letting me go out this weekend, and would you care to accompany me? I know a place where there is lots of enjoyment to be had."

"Why, Bone, I'm touched. Of course I'd like to accompany you. But how could it be arranged?"

Vast smile. "I got friends here, man."

"It was the craziest thing you ever saw," Rand was saying later on.

The story had made Phillips nearly hysterical.

"And what's more he sat there for the rest of the performance as though nothing had happened!"

Phillips bent over again, gasping. "Oh, no, please, you're killing me. Stop."

"So help me."

Then suddenly, as he was in the thick of recollection, it came on, the great noonday wail, throughout the entire city. To Rand it was a double sound: for one, a giant warning to the city's populace of approaching death from the love blue skies, but for the other it always struck him much more deeply, inescapably, as the city's collective scream, as though, once a day, at an officially appointed hour, all the citizens simultaneously opened their mouths and screamed out the agony and unendurable despair of their lives, and that this served as a release quite as effective as would the ritual of murdering a chosen victim to propitiate gods; a scream sustained for fully half a minute, a scream to God, and this too was a warning, for what this warned of could not possibly be escaped by ducking into cement holes in the ground.

Finally, it stopped, and Rand felt better, his throat muscles relaxing from the intense empathy just experienced.

Phillips was looking at him quizzically. "What's the matter?"

"Nothing."

"You're white. Sick?"

"No. That damned air-raid siren catches me unawares."

"So what happened after that?"

"Just anticlimax, of course," Rand answered, as from a distance. "He explained—or confessed—that he'd been asleep at Margaret's house. Then as soon as the curtain dropped, he beat it home."

Phillips shouted with pleasure. "I'll be damned." He knew he would get many hours of pleasure in fantasy reconstruction of Margaret and Hawkins. It would give fine play to his connoisseurship.

"But it's more reasonable than one would first think," Phillips resumed, more soberly. "They—the Negroes—are so bourgeois, you see, and this Hawkins is about the most bourgeois imaginable. So it's a perfect way for Margaret to attack, almost without knowing it, a bourgeois world she comes from and hates so savagely. In a way, eat her cake and throw it up too."

Rand had conceded that tricky possibility. Some of those thoughts his too.

"Natural-born Republicans—all of them," Phillips smiled slyly. "Makes it a most interesting perversion, doesn't it?"

The frigid face of Rand's wife appeared there in the doorway momentarily and she said au revoir to them both before descending to the market place. And immediately afterward both Phillips and Rand exchanged conspiratorial glances.

But about what? Rand asked himself. About the situation here with her? or about Janine? Does he know something? I shouldn't have made love to her, should have waited longer.

"You don't see Margaret any more, do you?" he asked Phillips on sudden inspiration, to take Phillips' mind off what he thought it was on: his affair with Janine.

Very quick of him, Phillips thought. Very.

"I see her, but in no special way. She's too jet-propelled now for me."

But he did not want to keep this bit about himself and Margaret afloat. Margaret with a middle-class Negro was interesting, but not himself and her. And then, in an unexpected avalanche, utter boredom with all goyim crashed over him, goyim white, goyim black, green or blue. Who invented those goddamn people anyway? He wailed. Manic children . . . they'll destroy the world yet. How did they get so dumb! Cheesy amebic insights. . . . Why don't they find out where they're going, for Christ sake? If it weren't for analysis. . . . He sobbed inwardly and asked to be among Jews now, comforting, wise, worldly, ancient and mellow. What am I doing here! I don't want to go to Minnesota; I want to go to Israel. Give Minnesota back to the fascists. God how I wish I knew Yiddish! I'd sing to myself in it for the rest of the day. Perfect. He remembered his own bar mitzvah and the nostalgic richness, sweetness, *realness* of it strengthened and warmed him here in this gentile barrenness. To hell with this Puritan Arctic! His groin was cold with it, his soul chilled.

After Phillips had gone, Rand immediately phoned Janine, and he kept one ear cocked for the nasty click-click of his wife's footsteps in the outside corridor. The thought of being surprised by that soured egret made his stomach twitch.

"Yes, yes," he whispered, "tonight, at about nine. All right, at your place. I have to go now. Good-by."

He was just sitting down to the newspaper when she returned. His eye caught an item about a huge endowment just created. Why couldn't he swing something there? Couldn't he think up a project they would endow? Schizophrenic patterns in Cherokee culture? History of twelve-toned chromosomes among the Mormons? Right next to this column was a paragraph, the sort of spice the paper was usually peppered with, concerning a holdup in an uptown bowling alley. Seems the two men were led by a pistol-swinging girl. Rand wondered what kind she was, Annie Oakley? Bonnie Parker? and turned the page. And he also was thinking of an excuse to use to get away this

night. Perhaps he could say the movies. But which
one? *Jack the Ripper? The Return of the Space Blob?*

Phillips had walked outside and thence almost
directly into the soft loving arms of a kosher restaurant a block away. He was strangely frightened and he
sensed imminent persecution, now that he had, back
there in Rand's apartment, recovered himself and
become identified once more with the Jews, cost what
it may. He was a cool cookie, that Rand. Lacked
depth, that's why. All wrapped up in his own problems. No time left for the rest of the world. No generosity of the spirit. Why, he even seemed miffed when
I asked to borrow one of those classy striped ties of
his.

Phillips' fears and anxieties, his severe, sudden
alienation made him hungry—what was more desirable, then, than a real Jewish restaurant? It made
him think of his grandmother, on whose warm lap, in
whose fragrant kitchen, he had spent his delicate early
childhood. (He had been a very precocious nipper.
Talked at ten months.) Cookies and wonderful stories.
The restaurant, he thought now, would resemble her,
Baba would keep out the world's harsh, unleavened
cold. He bent his head into the wind to protect his
small face, and made for the restaurant down the
street.

7

HARRY HAD ONCE SAID to Margaret,
"Have you ever seen a glass smashed by a sound that
somehow, out of nowhere, the street or the sky, had
that glass's exact pitch? Well, that's the way I see you.
Running from place to place, situation to situation,
idea to idea, unconsciously seeking your exact pitch,
the hidden thing that will, *is waiting to,* destroy you.
And when you find it—*smash!* you'll disintegrate just
like that glass."

They—she and Phillips, Harry and his wife—
were driving back from a coast resort after a weekend together. She had dared Phillips to swim out
beyond the rabid surf with her, that was it, coward
that he was. And what was it Phillips had angrily said
later, when she taunted him for his passivity? "A Jew
is a cageful of wild beasts. Don't forget that." Locked
cage though; at least his cage is.

But why was Harry always saying these things to her? What was he doing, putting the finger on her?

What a way to spend the morning! Margaret decided. Thinking about all that old garbage. Recalling her do with Hawkins had brought it all on. I must do something good today, and that's all there is to that. For somebody else, an act of kindness, human sympathy. Even if it is premeditated it's better than nothing—isn't it? She looked down at her naked thighs, rubbing them appraisingly with both hands. Fat, ought to thin down some. Beginning to look like a Dutch peasant. But they're nicer to feel when they are like this. Dilemmas. Hawkins—does he think they're too fat? Grandmother Arabella, I experienced a Negro on this very bed. A big black panther with a long wiry beard sprang upon me from the forests of the night. Ha! Not exactly the way it was but. . . . Suddenly, and with a faint thrill, her thighs remembered him. Ooo! Trembling. . . .

Visit Carter Barrows! That would be the good deed.

Have meant to for such a long time—sincerely wanted to but didn't; too confusing or something. But now, today!

And with that Margaret hot-showered gaily, for the crouching hostile day seemed routed.

"Margaret, what have you been up to? Or down to, should I say."

"Not much really, to tell you the honest truth, Carter."

"And that's exactly what we want, around here, Margaret—the honest truth. Do you have any idea what the truth is?"

"Why, uh, I'm afraid. . . ."

"Just as I thought. You don't have the remotest idea what it is."

"You're being awfully unpleasant, Carter. Why? I came here to. . . ."

"Good old Margaret, rich old Margaret. What lies have you been telling yourself lately? What little tricks have you been pulling?"

"What do you mean by that! Are you crazy?"

"Crazy as crazy can be. Don't you wish you were? It'd be the most definite thing that ever happened to you."

"Oh please, can't we be friendly? Do we have to. . . ."

"Do you remember the time you got drunk and tried to kill yourself in your bathroom with one of Phillips' leftover Gillette blue blades? Remember?"

"No! No!"

" 'Life was too much with you.' You stupid bitch! It wasn't enough with you. That's the whole trouble, don't you know that?"

No!

That's exactly the way it will go, I know it will. He hasn't changed a bit, he can't have.

Thus fearfully convinced, on her way up there to see him, she abruptly turned off the highway and fled back toward the center of the city. And she now began to cry a little; the strain and reality of the dialogue with herself had worked its way. After a while she calmed down, felt better, but it was of course out of the question that she would visit Carter. Another time perhaps, with somebody else along. There still remained, however, her original determination to perpetrate a good deed this day. What? Who? Where? How?

Had it *always* been so barren and desperate? she asked of her memory. Wasn't there a time when it was different, when despair was something other people talked about, like the diseases of the poor? Even when she was but a dainty of a girl, didn't she feel absolutely wonderfully sure then that life was her bluepoint? And wasn't she simply suffocated by love and attention? Winnie the Pooh and all that? *Please, please!*

Nope.

Ice tongs, that's what they handled me with. Never remember being touched, never given hugs and squeezes and sweet feels. Did I have leprosy, or were

they both amputees? Cold, cold, that's the way it was.
I finally did feel like the ice cube they were handling
me like. Hold me! Hold me! What did they do with
their lips besides purse them? ("My dear, don't you
know you don't have to slam doors in order to close
them?") Freezing. May I warm myself at your fire?
Yours? Yours?

But didn't I love my youth, the sweet lutelike spring-
time of my life? But memory failed, could only
produce concrete images of people and places and
things, no fantasy third dimension, no background
music, no temperature. No. All she had longed for
was to quickly grow up, achieve the freedom of
womanhood. In other words, *be what she was now!*
Oh God!

She had to stop now for a red light. That good
deed: what? Scanning the sidewalks while waiting . . .
dozens of bony Puerto Rican children scrabbling
raucously in tenement street play, chirping in their
odd bird voices . . . then, yes! She had it. A Spanish
family—that was it. One of those thousands of anti-
fascists hiding out in dismal sanctuary in the south
of France. She would go immediately to their head-
quarters here (from whence the recent mail appeal)
and sign up a family's needs for the winter. *Her*

persecuted family! *Her* starving children! Sister
Margaret!

And her Packard leaped forward joyously, liberated.

Not only that, but he gave me the letter besides!
Janine was still shocked by this act of Carter's.

Incredible, simply incredible. And they were going
to let him out soon? Don't they have any idea what
he's like?

But this suggested itself: Maybe he did it on purpose, for the amusement, to see what effect it would
have. That would be something like his old self; but
even that would be better than his not knowing what
he was doing. Or would it? What purpose the breakdown?

They're holding him prisoner!

And now here I am carrying around a message
from an insane man and I don't even have enough
courage to throw it away or brains to know *what* to do
with it. Plus the eerie fact that it has no stamp on it.

The obvious tricky, crazy problems lying ahead
made her grit her teeth in repressed anger. *Did he do
this on purpose? Did he?* To persecute me? If I do
put a stamp on the goddamn thing that means nothing
less than belief, and that. . . .

Why did I marry Carter? I can barely remember what he was like before this. In a way I must have been at fault. I mean, I don't think I married him primarily because he was such a great human being. He was always sort of erratic, as they say. Had other reasons. I was a stenographer and he was my boss, in those dear dead days almost beyond recall. But that wasn't entirely it. I think it was that I wanted to be married to a man of quality instead of to just an ordinary man.

Do I know what I mean?

Some idea I had about life being richer, more rewarding under those circumstances. An ordinary man can give you only affection and understanding. But I guess I didn't think that was enough. How wrong can you be? I wanted a person with pretensions. What is the magical difference between being beaten up by a duke rather than a milkman? Please tell me if you happen to know.

I must tell him. I must make him understand I'm through. He'll have to be strong enough to take it. Damn this coddling.

"Tear it up," said Rand. "That's the only rational thing to do, honey."

"I can't," she replied in quick defense of her new postal trust. Strangely, it seemed almost an assault, somehow, for Rand to be so decisive. Tearing up the letter would be like tearing up . . . tearing up Carter. No!

"I can't do that," she repeated. "It . . . it wouldn't be right."

Of course she wouldn't, he thought. How stupid of me to suggest it. Sooner bite off her thumb. It isn't love, I don't think; it's guilt about him that does this to her. Guilt much stronger than love, any day, and I should certainly know that.

They had indeed gone to a movie (Mickey Rooney as a crooked gas-pump jockey) and were now walking away from it (in Janine's neighborhood, of course, where there would be no chance of anyone spotting him, a la FBI). Would his baby son years from now sit up nights sticking needles into a wax effigy of him, the father, for what he was doing with Janine, for betraying his future, for considering abandoning his mother? That's the risk you take. Would the boy necessarily have to grow into some kind of cripple, ghoul, because he did not have the presence of a father? Why must he pay so heavily for a simple act of what could be called self-preservation? Haven't I the unalienable right to the pursuit of if not happiness surely less agony? God, what if Janine and Carter had a child!

"Of course," he said, taking Janine's arm, "You don't have to decide right now what to do with it. Give yourself time."

"I know, but for some strange reason it seems so urgent, crucial," and she shook her head in perplexity.

"What a fluky thing!" he said, seeing the humor of it, and this made them both break through with a noise resembling laughter.

Janine was very tired, she had been working hard all day, and she wanted some coffee. They were on the brink of entering a large cafeteria when Rand suddenly saw Hawkins sitting at one of the tables inside.

"No!" he whispered, and turned Janine away quickly. "It's the Negro."

"Did he see us?"

"I don't think so. I hope not." And he was in a panic to run.

They scurried rapidly up the street to a smaller place, a drugstore, and ducked in there.

"I hate this," Janine said, as they sat down in the back booth.

"I know, I know. I'm terribly sorry, honey." Then he added, "And running from of all people *Hawkins*."

"Would he betray us do you think?"

"I can't think how or to whom," Rand replied reflecting. "But the thing is that he *could,* assuming he saw us. What a peculiar power for *him* to have."

And they both sat quietly for a few moments thinking about this.

"What's he *doing* up here?" Janine asked, her voice edged sharply, as though he had no right or else had lost his way.

The question was too complex, too baffling, too ordinary for Rand at this moment, and he could only shrug to show that it was quite beyond solving right now. Please, just hot coffee, no more. That's the limit of my capacity.

After the coffee and a pastry (the fright of Hawkins since banished), Rand said, quite softly, like a very young child asking a delicate favor of an adult, "Have you ever thought of going to Haiti?"

For *shame,* for *shame,* Hawkins was murmuring to himself, coffee cup held above dark beard. What are they *thinking* of me? What are they *saying* about me?

It was because I was drunk. That damn Margaret made me. But Rand, bless him, had been sweet and most understanding. Giving the ushers that money— a stroke of genius. I must make it up to him. A true unblemished Christian. Obviously they had not all been eaten by the lions.

Fabulous party we had though, he recalled. The things she made me say to her! Lawsy! He would have blushed then and there, and he looked around to see if anyone was by any chance watching him. (Then he rested his arm comfortingly on the notebook in which he had been making notes for his lectures at the university, coming up very soon.) Made me *do* too!

Fascinating how these depravities show up in seemingly the most unlikely places. The woman was a veritable Barnum and Bailey sideshow.

Oh well, so long as it's all just in fun.

Fun, when was the last time he'd had any? Not pleasure, nor enjoyment, they were quite different. Fun, you know, penny-candy-greedy—unthinking— let's-do-it-again kind of thing. Long time no have. Ever? Let's see . . . oh yes . . . himself and a lad named Roach, Huby Roach, early in junior high school before he discovered the lands beyond the sea and heard the literary sirens calling. On Saturdays he and Huby drove around and around in an old model A Ford that Huby had bought for fifteen dollars. They'd take sandwiches and, on stolen gas, just ride in and out of the city, like young lords, or they sneaked into ball games and prize fights. And they used to laugh hysterically at the stupidity and strangeness of white people. Knocked them out. No white boys would mess with Huby because he'd break their ass if they did. He

was a natural-born tiger hunter and sweet as honey.
Halloo out there, Huby! he shouted across the misty
years. No answer. Ah well, everything changes, he
tried to tell himself. Laws of nature.

Hawkins was through and about ready to go, but he
paused momentarily to take in a conversational fragment from another table. Pure Brooklynese. To him
it was jewel-like. Just like Elizabethan street talk.
(The comparison made him like himself.) The Bard
would have loved it. That sort of thing should be recorded, as is, saved for posterity by the Library of
Congress. They did it for the hill-billy ballads, didn't
they? What's the difference? He decided to discuss it
with his class. This thought brought up another vision.

"Professor Hawkins, do you think the time of great
playwrighting has passed?"

"Yes, I'm afraid I do, Peterson."

"Would you tell me why, sir?"

"Audiences have lost their belief in, or sense of,
magic. In the old days they would identify themselves
so closely with a play that they really became partici-
pants. Today, because of oversophistication, we're
only spectators. Too bad, isn't it? We can't suspend
our disbelief quite enough."

"I think I see what you mean."

Outside the cafeteria, looking around before pointing his toes homeward, Hawkins noticed a letter al-

most at his feet, somehow fallen behind the fire
hydrant at the edge of the cafeteria building. Picked
it up, thinking of himself in that moment as a scav-
enger. Dr. Theodore Stevens, 185 Park Place. No
stamp. Should I?

"I'm being held here against my will, as a prisoner. . . ."

He finished the letter and did not know what to do
now. How had it found its way out of the asylum?
Certainly could not have done it by itself. Spooky.
He couldn't decide what to do, so he slipped the letter
into his bloated Elizabethan notebook to reconsider
later.

"As if we were not all being held prisoner," he
muttered, and started walking toward his apartment
around the corner, where he had but recently moved,
from the all-Negro quarter that clung by its shiny
fingernails to the periphery of the city, peeking in. It
was not even certain how long he would last there, for
the landlord, vacationing out of the city, did not know
that Hawkins had moved in. A white friend—a student
—had turned the apartment over to him rather on the
q.t.

"Everybody bend over!"

The orderly waited sternly while his command took
effect.

All the patients in the barnlike green room bent
over, frightfully, grotesquely unprotected below their
little green jackets, as though waiting for a giant razor
strap to shriek down on them in a communal whipping
for their sin of insanity, making them perverse, demented little boys rather than in any way adults
broken asunder. Though they did give off, in their
frozen, mute way, this expectancy of cruel punish-
ment of reprisal that boys muster in crucial moments
of this order. Carter too, with Bone Livingston and
Groz flanking.

"Okay."

An orderly walked down each row of frozen nudes,
and into each plunged a thermometer, greased, thank
God, but not enough, however, for here and there a
bending patient to hold back a squeal, a murmur, a
gasp of sharp pain.

In spite of all, Carter was amused. He could not
banish from his mind a childhood image of inserting
a firecracker thusly in neighborhood boys he did not
like. But this, in here, was for reasons of health, not
revenge. State of mind, state of body, and vice versa.
But still, what a way to start the day! The seconds
ticked by and muscles ached all over in protest. Some
heads raised to observe their fellow sufferers, others
kept theirs down in dignity's last chance.

It's an absolutely revolutionary way of gauging your psyche. You're 97.6 crazy this morning, old bean.

In another minute I'm going to fall on my face laughing, Carter thought, but their minute was up and the orderlies returned and reprieved them by plucking from each bent bum the jutting, offending stick of glass.

"That's it!" one barked, and all the men collected themselves, hurriedly, embarrassed (for now they could afford to be.)

Bone and Groz, still flanking, walked with him to the mess hall for breakfast. Carter had the feeling that little Groz wanted to slip inside his pants pocket for comfort and sanctuary. But Bone, on the other side, was a tall upright column of courageous black, smiling and clear-eyed, striding purposefully through life (despite the fact that Carter had several times heard from the guards that Bone was officially regarded as the very soul of insanity).

"Did it get through all right?" Groz asked of his letter.

"For the second time, yes," Carter replied. He'd be so much happier, better off, this Groz, if he were a baby squirrel. Too bad.

"I know you hate doing this," whined Groz. "You hate me, all of you."

I refuse to play that depraved game this morning.

Bone turned for no particular reason and presented Carter with one of his great smiles. It was Love itself, that smile. And Carter swiftly grabbed hold of it and let it carry him away, to Harlem, where they had sneaked to. Black, black—God, it was delicious. Those people certainly know how *not* to live. And the women —ah, the women!—still slaves, thank the *bon dieu*, to femininity. I kiss the memory of you, Louisa whatever-your-last-name is. May you never get a scholarship to Bennington. 'Twould be the end of you. They don't lie to their reflexes. White women—no names, please—even though they'll enjoy something, have to put up resistance first. Require pursuit or conning. Just to make you feel ratty. Nuts to that, kiddo.

"He'll have to help me," Groz whined. "His duty to mankind."

I'm not going to talk to him any more this morning, Carter decided.

Groz kept staring at him wistfully.

"It was real nice, huh?" said Bone as they sat down to chow.

"Golden fried chicken and rich whisky," Carter replied with true affection. "Every last bit of it."

"I have some more plans that I would like to discuss with you sometime in the near future. Important stuff."

"Let's make an appointment this very moment, Mr. Bone."

"Made?"

"Made, sir."

Someone at a far table shouted:

"A boob in the bin is worth two in the bush!" and laughed wildly, like a loon on a night pond.

From the lunatic clatter in the crowded mess hall Carter escaped into his diary.

"They all envied me, that's why they had me put here. Who can envy a man in the crazyhouse? To save *themselves* they did it."

He had written that in the first phase of his involuntary residence here. It was slightly different now, his point of view though, again, at times it backtracked, just, it seemed, out of caprice. But then all animals, or wild things, broke training suddenly that way: Hunting hawks, babies, white mice, prize fighters.

"It stinks. The inhumanity of the entire thing. What is man in all this?"

That had been his latest entry—almost, one might say, the opposite side of the above coin.

"Failure of belief must have been the reason I'm here now, otherwise why would any one wish to leave a world, or anything else, that he believed in? Question before the accused is, how to regain Belief *and in what*. Without that there is simply no point in accused leaving present address. One is not required to have anything here except a pulse. In the place I left, outside, living without belief is even crazier than it is in here, and I know. At what point did I lose it and why? That's what must be discovered. The fatal fork in the road.

"Janine, Rand, Phillips, Harry—what are they up to? 'When skies are hanged and oceans drowned, the single secret will still be man.' Do they know that?"

The lukewarm oatmeal he was spooning into his mouth seemed like the tasteless, unworked, primary protoplasm of all life. What everything was born with, what everything would destroy. At this moment he felt like throwing it into Groz's teensy face, foul teensy face that from one point of view was the apex of evolution and from another the absolute nadir.

Something very funny took place that afternoon. Phillips came to see him. "As I live and breathe," gasped Carter mockingly.

"Right. Touch me. I'm real," replied Phillips, shyly smiling at his own presence.

"You think."

"Okay, okay. I see you haven't changed," he said, a bit hurt by Carter's sharp remark.

"*I* have, but my method hasn't."

I think he *has* changed, mused Phillips. He never sounded that precise before.

"I brought you something," Phillips began. "A book."

Carter did not feel in the least grateful. He thought it was a cheap gift, and a disappointment.

"So I see," he said. "Yes," he went on, holding it up. "It's a book all right."

After they had been stretched out on the undulating greensward for a while, Carter abruptly asked, "Why did you come to see me?"

Phillips thought of several answers—answers glib and suave, flowery and enticing, like a wall full of rioting honeysuckle, answers with great style.

"I don't know," he confessed aridly. "I think I came just to look at you, Carter old boy."

(He had wanted, suddenly and quite strongly, to see what *it* was like, in somewhat the same way that scholars find it necessary to finger the ruins of Greek temples in order for them completely to comprehend, thereby, Greek history.)

"Zoo-like?"

"Afraid so."

"Well," sighed Carter, "at least there's something almost charming in that. I'd be lying if I tried to tell you I don't get somewhat the same sort of pleasure out of being insane that a giant baby panda gets out of being itself. On *one* level anyway."

He paused, searching for something, even a grass blade or a twig would do.

"Now what would you like to talk about?"

"You've got me, Carter."

"You didn't come prepared? No list of questions from the Student Council?"

"Nope. You see, I didn't consider this from the conversational angle."

"That's only too apparent," observed Carter. "But what do you say we give it a try—just for the hell of it?"

"I'm game."

"Splendid! Now let's see . . . hmm . . . how about the weather?"

Phillips shook his head.

"I can't think of a single thing to say about it," he admitted looking Carter up and down.

Carter thought for a moment.

"I've got it. Let's talk about you."

"Ooo!" Phillips winced. "Perish the thought. Man. It would be too grim."

"I see what you mean," sympathized Carter. He was quiet for a minute, trying. "Well," he sighed in defeat, "I guess that does it, eh?"

"An unavoidable conclusion," agreed Phillips, getting up preparatory to leaving.

They looked each other over—Moon Man examining Venus Man—utterly confirmed in their mutual failure, shook hands and parted. Phillips had gone only a very short way when Carter, ran after him shouting:

"Wait! Take this!"

Phillips looking puzzled, stopped and turned around.

"Take what?"

"This," gasped Carter, and dropped a handful of grass into Phillips' jacket pocket.

"What?"

"A memento, a souvenir. Like a chip off the Colosseum, to show you've really been there. Bon voyage!"

With that, Carter strode away, toward the building, leaving Phillips to figure his own way out.

Carter gave the book to one of the male nurses, who had oodles of time to waste.

8

8

THERE THEY WERE—Harry and Hawkins together, and in Hawkins' apartment to boot.

"I can't understand why you'd like to meet him, Hawkins," said Harry of Phillips. "He's really no better than a common thief. Worse, in fact. He steals other people's ideas the way a robber burgles houses. Why, would you believe that in the last year alone that bastard has filched no less than three ideas from me? Major ones, too. One of them was the only original contribution to psychoanalytic theory since Harry Stack Sullivan. It was a new approach to problem children."

He paused to catch his breath and shake his head in wonder at Phillips' monstrousness.

"The awful thing is that there's no law protecting society against such as he. He should be as punishable

154

as the burglar. Three to five years in Sing Sing, that's
what he should get. Make it a felony, by God."

Hawkins, at this moment, felt just like a person in
love; the delicious, ginger-ale-like physical sensation
was quite the same. And why not? This was where his
real passion lay, in the intellects of and acceptance by
men like Harry; this was where he would be or not be,
This was true soul-mating, compared to which a little
sordid scuffling with the likes of Margaret was gnat-
small in meaning. At least, that is what he was now
telling himself as he listened to Harry.

Harry had come to see Hawkins after Rand told
him about the man. "He has genius," Rand had said
ambiguously.

And Harry wanted to find out what he had it for.
Because genius, like freedom, only existed in relation
to something specific. It has no resemblance, whatever, to plankton and anybody who thinks so is
cracked. So in his own calculated way Harry was
circling round and round Hawkins looking for his
genius denominator.

"I'd love to have you lecture to my class sometime,"
confessed Hawkins. "Would you? Just on things in
general, the cultural climate and so on."

"I come high, Hawkins, very high," Harry warned
him. "Which reminds me. I'm not going to any more

parties like the Johnses'. Not unless I'm paid, like an
entertainer, which I am as far as they're concerned.
My fee will be fifty bucks per. That's peanuts compared to what Danny Kaye pulls down."

"But I can't. . . ."

"For you it will be less. That is, if I decide to do
it. I'll let you know."

"Of course," Hawkins said politely, not knowing
whether to consider this last outburst soberly. He
wasn't quite sure whether Harry was kidding him or
not. (For what lover, in his caressings, can or will
call a clay foot just that when he gropes for it?)

"What were the other ideas that Phillips filched
from you?" asked Hawkins eagerly, to distract Harry
from the subject of money.

Harry was beginning to see his man more clearly
now. Yes, he thought he knew what Hawkins' genius
was, and the discovery was quite gratifying too. It
fitted in perfectly with his new project.

"The relation of urban intellectual man to contemporary society for one," began Harry, watching
the fascinated gleam come into Hawkins' eyes, feeling Hawkins' yearning vibrations. Easy as giving
candy to a baby, he thought, as he began to weave
the web. Hawkins, he knew now, the dazzling words

spinning out from his mind, spider-like silver strands, had a genius for being corrupted. It was his destiny.

That previous evening the project had been hit upon by Harry and Shanley. A stroke of luck, to be exact.

"This kid Joey said she was a real weird one and a lush besides," reported Shanley. "She gives him twenty bucks to put on a whiz-bang for her with some little neighborhood piece. Something, huh?"

"What's the dear lady's name and where in this stupendous city does she reside?" he asked.

Shanley reached into a pocket. "I wrote it down. Here it is," he said, pulling from his pocket a dirty piece of paper. "Margaret Lansing. 125 Darrow Street. Apartment 4A."

Ooo la la! And Harry began to laugh and stamp his foot with surprise and uncontrollable pleasure. I knew it! I knew it! I knew it! Whoever invented the circle really knew what he was doing. Oh Momma!

"What's the matter?" asked Shanley, squinting suspiciously at his friend Eddie Brien.

"Man! Man!" cried Harry.

Then he came out of it. "Nothing. I just saw them all in that whiz-bang and it broke me all up."

"Yeah," said Shanley, no longer puzzled. "So this

is the deal, Eddie," and Shanley's jackal face became taut with desire and intent as he outlined the project. It could not have been lovelier had the Bard himself schemed it.

One thing you had to say about Shanley: he liked his work. He wasn't swimming against the tide like a lot of people.

And after their conference they picked the girls up to fool around a little. Poor Mac, he was sick, it turned out (something wrong with his tummy), and it was then that Harry thought of Hawkins as an ideal substitute for Mac on their project. At first Shanley didn't like the idea one little bit; his neighborhood-trained dislike of Negroes, and all that. But he finally said okay when Harry told him of certain fine, pleasurable, and criminal things this Negro—he said he was an elevator operator—was privy to in his own moonlit world and could later on, as a reward for including him, share with them. It was all set then.

Edna was sweet. "I got you something," she told him.

"Yeah? What?"

"You'll see when you come up."

And she kissed him there in the bar, where they'd gone for a beer or two.

What she had bought him Harry could not have

liked more. It was an exuberant and astonishingly vulgar tie. But here in this context it was in exquisite
taste, and the gift itself was the most felt one he had
received from anyone since he was a small boy. While
Shanley and Myra discreetly went into the other room,
Harry made love to Edna, and it was such a real and
intimate experience for her—and, she sensed, for
Eddie too, else no reality for her—that she cried a
little afterward. It was adorable, and Harry loved it.

"Let's get us a place together," she suggested.

Harry had foreseen this but had no satisfactory
solution to it at this time. He didn't know how it could
be brought off, not that he didn't want to do it.

"I want to think about it, honey," was his answer
for the time being.

Edna found this acceptable.

When Harry finally left Hawkins he carried away
with him two things: Hawkins' most enthusiastic reaction to the scheme, and also Groz's letter. Harry
(both of them carried high by a few glasses of Roberta
Johns's favorite poet Johnny Walker) had presented
the scheme to Hawkins in an irristible fashion. The
whole thing was an ideal concretization of poetics and
philosophy. Hawkins had uncontrollably winced upon
hearing of Margaret's compounded depravity, but his

delight at Harry's dual existence was so great that he had to restrain himself from embracing the man.

The letter—he had gladly given it to Harry to mail when Harry, seeing it on a table, inquired into its identity, then said it would amuse him to send it on its way.

He did too. At home he slit the letter open (for Hawkins had resealed it as if to say "You can't prove I opened this letter.") and read it—Groz's mad plea for help. Of course he had to send the poor man a reply. Only fair.

"My dear Groz:

Your ingratitude is absolutely shocking. And after all we have done in your behalf too. I know dozens of perfectly rational people who would give their right leg to be in your shoes. So for goodness sake, stop this idiotic yowling about freedom. Stay where you are! You're sitting pretty!

Enviously yours,
Segismundo Freud"

Phillips' mouth touched the girl's ear.

"Your conversation reminds me of a Bach fugue, baby. You add something to speech, some strange musical pattern. No kidding."

He had thought of this image some time ago and had been patiently waiting for an opportunity to

launch it. Ears, he loved them. They were such perfect little receptacles. Tasty, too.

"Mmm, that's *beautiful*," the girl murmured. "Tell
me something else like that."

"Greedy little thing, aren't you?"

"As if *you* weren't!"

Women and the arts—he couldn't do without them.
If he wasn't indulging in the one, he was indulging
the other. They were really so much alike, too; or at
least there was some connection between them. And
food, don't leave that out. Often when he felt bad,
lonely or anxiety-bugged, his first (instinctive)
solution was to read a book, or get laid, or have something yummy to eat. And sometimes, praise the Lord,
he wished he could do all three at the same time.

Suddenly he was reminded of an observation of
Harry's re homosexuals and culture.

"Have you ever known a fag who wasn't listening
to symphonies, or looking at paintings, or reading
books? Frustrated, cut off, inorganic, they use the
arts as bridges of love. It's their way of making connection with each other."

"What has that to do with me?"

"Just this. You're impressed by this hoax. Your
love of the the 'arts' is going to turn you into an awful
goof one of these days, if you don't watch out."

Very provocative, Harry, though I don't think he's

Nostradamus. Have to call him up for a drink soon.
Should see more of each other probably. Though he's
gotten a trifle mysterious lately. But who hasn't? Who
hasn't? It's the pressures on a man. Money, if he
didn't get some soon, well, he didn't know what he
would do. No answer yet from that well-to-do-know-
nothing he had written to. Patience, patience. But one
cannot wait forever, that myth about us to the contrary. Even the Jews finally have a time limit.

Maybe that wild man Hawkins could get me a
spoonful or two of the academic gravy. Worth a try.
Imagine that Rand slipping it to Barrows' missus!
Man's best friend *is* a dog after all. Ha! What a world.
Too bad I'm not hungry all the time, then I could eat
constantly. Hope this sweet thing offers to rustle up
a little grub for poppa-daddy soon. Then maybe a
good movie. When it's very dark and cozy, like in a
movie, I don't feel lonely. Why is that? Should write
a movie called *I Stuffed a Teen-age Derma.*

She moved her unabashed young legs.

"How are you doing?" Phillips asked.

"I'm waiting for some more sweet talk."

"What? Oh yes. Sure, why not," and he began to
whisper something very unusual to her, for she was
still virtually a child and did not yet believe in the
reality of words.

Margaret was licking lots of white envelopes, and with each lick she thought she was unsealing a fate. It was this Spanish refugee business, and Margaret, having acquired this new luxury, was writing to all her acquaintances begging them to come across with a little cabbage for these unfortunate people who otherwise would undoubtedly finally become victims of fascist logic.

"Save them!" she demanded of Phillips, Harry, Rand, Janine, Hawkins, Freda, the Johnses and several others. "*Save them!*"

She was miffed, for just a second, that insanity prevented Carter Barrows from getting one of her letters. Damn him.

Each letter seemed to Margaret a fresh, eager root which she was sinking from her body into the loam of existence, making her truly organic. This thing she was doing was meaningful, related her to history.

(At this moment she simply would not have been able to comprehend the word *luxury* had it been thrown in her lap like a soft orange.)

Now then, Hawkins—she had decided she wanted to marry him, and very soon too. This would be the realest act of her life, she thought, could undo all past error, banish from the future all judgments of frivolity.

"Do you hear that, Gran?" she shouted gleefully at the Silent Witness on the wall. And she stood still before the picture for moments listening to her yelling demand echo down Time's diminishing corridors.

They were going to have lunch, at her old school club. But she would not propose to him then, the daylight would be too harsh for such a soft scene. The night, the tender night, would be best for all concerned. "I'm developing photokinesis of the mind," she informed herself, and rather liked the idea.

Perhaps we could go to Switzerland for our honeymoon, and race down those heavenly white slopes, hand in hand, dark glasses protecting our tender vision, children of God.

But at lunch Hawkins was strangely elusive with her. She couldn't understand why.

"What's got into you anyway?" she wanted to know.

"Nothing, really," Hawkins lied delicately.

"Are you feeling strange because you're the only Negro here?"

"What a silly idea!" Pause. "Of course not." Pause. "I've a lot of class work, that's what is preoccupying me," he lied again. For seeing Margaret now, bathed in the ferocious light of Harry's revelation, was indeed unnerving, and utterly changed the reality of their odd relationship, strange episodic lovers that they were. In his mind was a picture of this frenzied, depraved woman entertaining and being entertained by Joey and the girls. It was a Frieze from the pornographic ruins of Pompeii.

Margaret, finishing off the chicken creole, wished she could spring the question now and forever calm the man, but she was determined to wait. (Wasn't it a wonderful scream the way her fellow club members were with polite surreptitiousness glancing at them in order to be goose-pimply shocked!)

"Oh!" Margaret gasped suddenly, "There's Rand's wife." And she waved to that marble-faced young woman as she sat down with a female friend. "I haven't seen her in *ages*. She never goes out any more."

This *was* worth talking about.

"Tell me about him," Hawkins asked her. As a gift of gratitude Hawkins had sent Rand an expensive illustrated edition of the *Canterbury Tales*. (With this inscription: "and I will friend you, if I may, In this dark and cloudy day.")

"Poor man," Margaret began. "He's awfully intelligent and sweet—but *so* unhappy. I don't think he ever quite recovered from a breakdown he had a few years ago."

"*He* broke down?"

"Oh yes. One summer when he and his wife were living in a summer cottage I owned on the coast. He was in a hospital for a short time and then he came out of it. Nobody knows of this except me and them. Now you. It was too shameful a thing to be public."

"Not even this man Barrows—the one who's crazy now, his best friend?"

"Nope, not even him."

"My God," muttered Hawkins. However, this awful secret, once sunk in, had the effect of endearing Rand to him even more, gave him a Lear-like dimension. Then what was this intense relationship with Carter Barrows that he'd heard about? What did it all mean?

"But don't you think somebody ought to tell Barrows?" Hawkins asked, in genuine anguish.

"No. Why?"

"Well, just to sort of clear things up." He really did not know why.

Margaret shrugged. It was all too remote for her now. She stared into her coffee grounds for some seconds.

"Hawkins—I mean Christopher—do you believe in me?" she suddenly asked him.

Hawkins automatically put his hand to his beard to steady himself. "Of course I do," he replied, concocting his third lie of the day. The next image that appeared to him, jack-in-the-box-like (and with such a face too), was Judas.

"You've become such an awful liar lately," she had snarled.

"Nonsense," Rand replied demurely to his wife, flicking through his Chaucer present.

"You're having an affair with someone and that's that. And it's probably someone I know, which makes it doubly humiliating."

"Please, please," he said wearily, for the very fact that it was true made it boring.

"Then how do you explain this?" she shrieked, and from a hidden clenched fist threw a handkerchief in his face.

He snatched at it, afraid, and saw the criminal lipstick stains—the same color as murder. Stupid of me! Imagine keeping it!

"Quite easily," he answered. "When I saw Harry yesterday I noticed that he had lipstick on his neck. So I gave him my handkerchief to wipe it off. Call him up and ask him, if you don't believe me."

"And even further degrade myself," she moaned.

"In that case, I'm afraid you'll have to take my word for it."

"Goddamn you!"

The hate-filled heels click-clicked into the far bedroom, and Rand thought of them as stalactites of horror. He sat quite still for a few minutes and tried to work the quarrel out of his system, sweat it through his brain pores. Such scenes made him feel jagged and used.

He had a sudden desire to see the child. The vision that purifies, be one ever so sullied. He walked criminally down the hallway and into the child's room. Smell and feel of sweetness there. Asleep. He looked down at him and silently soaked himself in this ambience. Being cleansed, calmed. He thought of a game they played.

"You be me, Daddy, and I'll be a naughty old witch and I'll pretend I'm eating you up."

"But no witch is going to eat you up. Who told you. . . ."

"Come on, Daddy. Play it, play it."

"All right."

"Grr, grr, I'm a witch and I'm eating you up!"

"Help! Help! Daddy, Daddy, a witch is eating me!"

Lots of giggles from the child. What do you think it means? Is some of the horror of this marriage rubbing off on him? Or is this just good clean psychodrama? Lizzy Borden took an ax and gave her father forty whacks. No, no. All this thinking was probably just a desire to punish himself. He bent down and kissed the child's cheek.

What made it so awful, he thought, returning to his chair, was that it was a hate quarrel and not a love squabble. Love can make you say and do the same things sometimes. And just what was it that made Carter do that to Janine? Love or hate?

"He suddenly grabbed me and forced me into this little workroom and made me do it," Janine had told him fearfully, just this morning. "Raped me. You've no idea how terrible it was," and the tears had trickled down to wash it all away. "He's positively dangerous."

Was it his love made him do that, or hate? Rand could easily see him doing it in hatred, and contempt too, if he strongly suspected Janine of betraying him. But he could not see him doing it in love, not in his condition; for his love was too deeply, inextricably, bound up in the mesh of his psychosis, was for *it* and not for humans, as Narcissus belonged to the mirror, was its exclusive property. This made Rand think, sadly, of the frequent sick alliance in his very own life, of sexuality and violence. The former a soft,

insidious leech on the other's wild energy, in a most
evil way calling violence forth, a genie, to perform
its own miracle, so lacking was it in true vitality.

"And they're letting him *out* soon," Janine went on,
held in his embrace. "Letting him out!"

It was then they came to the decision: to flee together to Mexico. After Carter got out but before he
settled back down inside her (they both assumed this
would be his intention), and at the same time Rand
would instruct his own demon to consult a lawyer.
Until then, of course, subterfuge was the only device
left to them. That stupid handkerchief! Stained,
bloodlike.

And another thing: he had seen Carter for the last
time, not only because of the wife-stealing but also
because it had personally become too much for him.
The identification with Carter must now be stopped, or
he must take Carter's place. He could not go on letting
Carter's breakdown be the unlived, unallowed extension of his own shrieking plunge into the Great
Abyss, from which he had so quickly returned.

"Shall we draw out our wits and duel?" Carter
asked as soon as he saw him last time.

"I'm defenseless," Rand told him, to stop the thing
right there.

"Even more than you know," snapped Carter with
a sharp ambiguousness.

Now what is he getting at? It's one of his down days, so I'd better tread carefully. But what about his treatment, doesn't it take? I don't quite remember. . . .

Carter was quite rambled that day, leaping from one thing to another, unable to decide just which peak or plateau he wanted to remain on. Rand leaped along with him, trying to keep a safe distance; however, something was up with Carter, but Rand did not know just what. Carter ravaged grass blades by the hundreds.

"Do you ever think what it was like to live in occupied France—as a Frenchman?" Carter shot out.

"Why should I, Carter? I mean. . . ."

"Every move, every thought watched by the enemy. The whole morality changed—your good moves recorded as bad, and vice versa. The city alive with treachery. . . . the very sidewalks turned traitor.

He seemed transported by this image and he acted as though he were at this moment with *it* rather than with Rand. Rand waited for him to return, but meanwhile, so passionate was Carter's vision that for seconds it became almost real for Rand too, and where the asylum's soft lawns were now, he saw a street quivering gently with an evil awareness, deserted except for the dark, haunted, uncertainly moving figure of one man—Carter, or himself. And he shuddered—then Carter returned.

"What was I saying?" he asked, confused. "What point was I making anyway?"

"Occupied. . . ."

"Oh yes! Well, that's the way it seems to me at times." He paused and confusion again sprinkled his face. "But I can't quite explain it."

"I think I understand," Rand told him, but he did not go into details.

"Do you?" Carter asked harshly, his hostility returned. "I don't see how you could, old boy."

"Then let's say that I get the general idea," Rand apologized, rather than offering proof of his identification.

Carter laughed cruelly at the feebleness of this gesture.

On their way back to the ward Carter smiled oddly at Rand and said, "I'm worried about you."

"Why?"

"Because you're buying property on a blind alley."

Don't argue even though you know he's needling you. "Any suggestions?"

"Next time," Carter mocked.

"Thank you, doctor."

Just as Rand was handing Carter over to those loving dark arms at the locked ward door, Carter's mood changed, as out of a flat, gray desert a twisting black tornado appears with murderous suddenness.

"What do you want here?" he screamed at Rand. The guard grabbed him as he screamed on, struggling in the doorway. "You robbed me of my freedom, you robbed me of my wife, and now you've come to rob me of the only thing I have left—my insanity! You lousy son of a bitch!"

And as Rand watched, stunned, speechless, the Negro guard wrestled Carter inside the ward and slammed the iron door on him.

Yes, he reflected now, Chaucer idle in his fingers, that was the final visit. From this point onward, it is every soul for himself.

9

ə

ONCE MORE, just one more time with Joey and the girl, Margaret thought, then tomorrow I'll propose to Hawkins, and my whole life will be different.

My whole life. . . . If I had it to live over again, what would I wish to be?

"I think it's simply wonderful the way you are able to come and go as you please," Roberta Johns told her the other day.

"I suppose so."

"Unlimited horizons."

"Uh-huh."

"You should thank you're lucky stars, sugar, that you're not tied down by a husband and a family."

"Should I?"

"Why of course you should."

"Okay. If you say so."

Mrs. Christopher Hawkins. The bearded prof's fair lady. Maybe I could help him start a clinic for the mentally retarded. Would he like that? Well, anyway, we could do *something* together. Research? My bank, his brains. What do they call children who are half white, half black? Quadroons? No. Mulattoes? I'll have to ask him. Wonder what he's doing right now? Is he happy? Ask him.

She was waiting for them now, and within her the stage was dramatically set. She was tight to just the proper degree. Nervously, she got up from her chair and walked in front of her grandmother's portrait. Was staring into it for something she might have been missing all this time, when the doorbell rang. All other thoughts then fled from her mind, fled fearfully as peasants in a square, suddenly hearing the sound of approaching Cossack hoofbeats, flee, leaving that place fabulously empty except for its passionate open-loined sensitivity, awaiting orgy.

Phillips gleefully picked up his phone and without bothering to dial a number shouted into it, to the world, "Hot diggity! I've got it."

"Ah loves ya, honey, ah loves ya," he murmured to the lovely green check. "I'll make you the best husband you ever saw," he promised it.

Furthermore, he was to appear at a stated hour at a railway station day after tomorrow. He would be met by a car and immediately driven to his new job. For just a second Phillips felt like a European refugee being transported by a committee to a new future in a new land. . . .

Cash it!

But since he did not have an account of his own (oh how the symbols crashed around him!), he had to have the necessary connections. Margaret too messy —besides, I still owe her the twenty; Rand whom he called—but Rand behaved very strangely, seemed angry to be thusly disturbed, said that he was up to his ears in something or other and just couldn't break free; so sorry he must have a very low degree of empathy. So it was to Roberta Johns that Phillips was driven. Which, when it was being an accomplished fact, was hard to take—he did not like to find her who had always been nonessential suddenly indispensable. It made him want to make pee pee.

The experience with the check was subtly changing a wheel here, opening a new valve there, half beknownst to Phillips, half not, and he made plans for his departure with a sudden slackening of enthusiasm. Begorra, the stink of it, a man like me jostled this way and that by the tides of society, when if they only knew it I'm the one can salvage them all.

For several crucial minutes Phillips had been standing in front of a travel office still absorbed in his musings, but now he opened his eyes and let rush in the various images of the bright travel posters. Italy! France! Spain! Greece! Michigan!

Michigan?

"No" he shouted. "I won't, I won't go there. Who do they think they are, ordering me around like that? Think they can own me a few lousy bucks, make me beholden to them. They're wrong! I'm not going to Michigan, Mrs. Money Bags, I'm going to Europe. That's where I belong. I'm going to walk with Voltaire, I'm going to see with Rembrandt, I'm going to sing with Homer. Michigan indeed!"

And Phillips resolutely strode into the travel office to make the necessary reservations for his historic odyssey. ("And the waves of the sea did pant for him," he sang aloud as the fatal door closed behind him.

"Thought they had me! *Me!*"

The beard was gone and in its place was the smooth round face of Jack Davis which was Hawkins' anonymous identity for the evening. Harry had done a bang-up job on him.

"It'll simply have to go," Harry explained to him. "You'd never get away with it with that thing on."

(Oh Hawkins, if you only knew what a mask your real face is! Harry had chortled to himself.)

So Hawkins, eager to do this thing in just the way Harry wished, shaved the beloved beard off, thus performing what Harry really wanted; that is, for Hawkins to unmask himself. (Hawkins, however, did not totally turn his back on himself. He shaved the beard off very neatly at the roots *and kept it* as though it were a falsie he had bought, which he might, who knows, stick back at some future time. Kept it in a little box, all glued together.) Not only that, he was wearing hoodlum clothes this night, to complete the role Harry had created for him. Precipitated him into a real neutral zone: Who was he now? He didn't have the faintest idea, to tell the honest truth.

"In a society which has no meaning, Hawkins, my boy, what could be a more appropriate gesture than ours?" is the succulent way Harry had put it to him.

"Quite," Hawkins replied in infatuation. He was far gone.

Harry had not of course explained to Hawkins his own special ironic reasons and pleasures in the whole thing, and especially in having persuaded Hawkins into it. He was ecstatic about it.

Now the three of them—Hawkins, Harry, Shanley and his sweet black pistol—were approaching Mar-

garet's building. They had been waiting in a doorway
across the street for the right moment, which was the
appearance, finally, of Joey and his girl, their bac-
chanal finished, leaving Margaret's walk-up and
quickly, because they knew what was to follow, scurry-
ing away (somewhat drunkenly) in the direction of
the subway and their own dark world. The girl was
buttoning her blouse.

"Let's get up there," Harry said softly to Shanley
and Hawkins.

"I can hardly wait," said Shanley, smiling in anti-
cipation.

"Me too," murmured Hawkins. He was almost shaking with fear and pleasure and strangeness.

Shanley could not help sharply glancing at the
Negro when he said this. Coming from him the "me
too" was charged and ambiguous and made Shanley
unsure, momentarily, that they both meant the same
thing.

Then all three silently agreed to move in, and they
hurried across the dark street and into Margaret's
apartment building.

Margaret was still in a swoon—lying nude on her
living-room floor, in superbly exhausted levitation. In
a sense she was still within the embrace of her dream-
like orgy, just passed, so that what was shortly to

happen was made, by her depraved apparatus, an extension of that dream and not outside it, just as, while in a true dream the real telephone at our bedside rings, our dream takes that sound and, to protect the sleep, cleverly incorporates it into the fabric of the story.

Thus it was that when, through her numbed senses she saw Shanley, Harry and Hawkins (they wore little black masks), sneaking into her apartment and whispering, it did not disturb her, because it seemed, momentarily at least, to be another phase of the extraordinary physical and psychological orgy with Joey and the young street girl. And just as a totally sated glutton will still flick an eyelash, move a feeble hand, and salivate when yet another tidbit is exposed to him, so Margaret's senses trembled with exhausted pleasure at this intrusion, as she lay coma-like on the rug, near the couch, her clothes ripped and scattered all around her, the whole room rank with evil whisky smell.

Surveying this debauched scene, still warm, as it were, the three masked marauders responded so quickly, so passionately to it that they were indeed, as it had been with Margaret, incorporated into that dream, and savagely participated in it. They attacked her on the floor, though they had not planned this.

Three mad wolves upon a snow-white lamb; a bit lushed, they were.

In the midst of it, Margaret came out of her dream state and in horror saw a masked Negro devouring her, and she screamed and began to fight for her life. Nothing else to do but smash her in the face to quiet her, and then they gagged her with her torn brassière. After him Harry, who, now raging with violence and desire, also beat her as he ravaged her. To say nothing of what Shanley perpetrated upon her helpless body. Dimly through it all, through her drunkenness, her confusion, her awful bruising beating, Margaret thought there was something familiar about two of the marauders, but this very thought only deepened the nightmare.

In the general madness, Harry gleefully decorated her apartment in a way he thought most fitting. He painted a mustache on Sargeant's stern portrait of Granny, and on the bathroom walls, employing a lipstick tube of Margaret's, he drew the sort of pictures and scribbled the inspired primitive filth customarily found only in public toilets. Names, telephone numbers, requests, specifications, capacities.

They left her unconscious and then ransacked her place, hurriedly. All three had completely lost their individual identities in the all-embracing criminality

of the situation and so were simply and truly nameless hoodlums, which in the fury and weirdness of it,
they each felt themselves to be, and would be until
they were well outside its aura.

Synchronized, they hurried out of Margaret's apartment when they had taken all her jewelry and money.
But as they entered the corridor outside they heard
the police charging up the stairs. Someone had heard
Margaret's screams and called them.

"The roof!" Shanley barked, and they raced up the
stairs and onto the roof, followed by the police.

It simply had to be that Shanley would use his
tense black pistol. As the police came out upon the
roof after them, and as Shanley, Harry and Hawkins
were crossing over to the next roof, Shanley turned
and fired upon them.

The police fired back. They dropped Hawkins first,
in the back of the neck. He spun around and momentarily faced the policemen.

"This isn't me!" he shouted to them, "this isn't
me!" then fell.

As he was dying, in that most amazing moment,
Hawkins returned to himself—returned through every
mask he had ever worn, every garment of deception
he'd ever hidden in, penetrating even the mad hood's
clothes he was now wearing—and just as he was about
to see, finally, who he was, he died.

Shanley and Harry made it to the roof entrance of the next building, and Shanley went in and Harry was behind, when the police got him, twice, in the back and in the side. He fell, as Shanley escaped to the world which was waiting for him open-armed, true son of it that he was, no dillier with identities, no dallier with self, a single dealer of infinite simplicity. And as Harry was succumbing, the entire mad adventure and its most tragic, ironic ending struck him as so superbly symbolically grotesque and just, so ludicrous, that he began to laugh. But it was not laughter that came out of his mouth; no, it was, instead, his own life's blood, darkly staining the dirty rooftop. He moved a finger in the blood and started to scrawl an obscene word, his last statement to the world, but before it was writ his life left him.

"If it ain't him, then who is it?" one cop asked the other, looking down at Hawkins, the Negro's great confessional shout still ringing in his ears.

"Don't ask me," the other cop replied. "If he don't know, how should I?"

Hawkins could have been identified and through him old Harry too, and both thereby saved from nameless graves in potter's field, by a letter that had fluttered unseen from his pocket, while he was running, and fallen down the air-way. The letter notified him that he was being dispossessed. But the police

did not see it, so it remained Hawkins' secret, forever
and ever.

Carter and Bone scaled the high iron fence by the
light of the moon and were then on their way. Escaped.

"Bone, you've liberated us," said Carter in praise
of Bone's clever maneuvering which had got them out.

"Nothing to it," replied Bone with the casualness
of the true magician.

"Listen, Bone," Carter began, as they entered the
seemingly neutral no man's land that lay between the
world behind and the world ahead, "I want to say that
knowing you has been one of the very few true experi-
ences of my adult life."

"Think nothing of it," said Bone the magician.
"Only wish you could see your way clear to accom-
panying me to Hollywood."

"Me too, but I've got a little business here to attend
to. At any rate, I'm counting on you to set Zanuck and
Goldwyn straight. Set them back on their true dream
path."

"Precisely. I've decided on my first picture: Ivan-
hoe."

"I'm with you, Bone, I'm with you all the way."

Remembering something, he took an envelope from

his pocket. Margaret's plea for help for the persecuted Spanish. Her unconscious had tricked her and sent it to Carter after all. No wall too thick, no person too remote.

"Give this to Zanuck, Bone," said Carter. "It's a scenario for a great new movie."

On first re-entering the city Carter had the feeling that he was stepping inside a jukebox, and for just a second his reflexes grabbed him and yanked him back toward the insane asylum. But this passed: he had so much to do. If one is to destroy the Devil, one must descend into Hell, is that not so?

It was not very long before they reached that plateau, in their joint descent from the peaks, where they had to go their private ways. Carter walked oddly, because inside his trousers he had a knife taped to his right thigh. Stolen from the butcher, back there in the asylum.

"*Vivere resolutamente!*" Carter cried, squeezing Bone's strong black hand.

"You too, man," Bone answered, gazing lovingly into his friend's tortured white face for a few seconds, then he vanished into the waiting night.

Carter rode a bus to his apartment—or the place he used to live. He would find and expose them tonight, Rand and Janine, show them that his suspicions were not paranoia after all. An awful struggle was being waged inside him, between his strange self and his not strange self, each trying to subdue the other and take absolute, dictatorial control. Do as *I* say! No! Obey *me!* So at one moment he decided to murder both Rand and Janine if he caught them, and at the next to treat them as nonexistent. His whole being strained with this fight.

From this bus stop to the apartment building was a full block, but so intensely, so intimately felt was the whole thing by Carter that, his eyes fixed hotly upon the building ahead, he actually tiptoed stealthily along the sidewalk from bus stop to building as if he were already creeping inside a dark sleeping bedroom. And he made not a sound as he climbed the back fire escape to the second floor. The lights were on in Janine's bedroom.

Throbbing madly now, Carter peeked in.

Yes! There they were, Rand and Janine in criminal embrace! And on the very bed that once was his sole preserve!

Kill! Kill! Kill! was screamed in Carter's horrified brain, and his vision was momentarily blurred and distorted by the pressure on him from inside and out. He furiously yanked the murder knife out of his pants.

Kill!

But then abruptly, climactically, as he was climbing onto the window ledge, something within him gave way, a flooding over, a bursting of held-down, frustrated tension, overwhelming almost to convulsion, and after this a tranquillity came to him that he had never felt before, a beatific, transcendent lucidity. Relieved, changed, he carefully laid the long knife on the window ledge where they would eventually discover it.

"For their cake or their throats."

He turned his gaze from the clutching pair inside (as they were grabbing at each other Carter grabbed at his soul), straightened up from his mad crouching position, and lovingly embraced the long tree limb that reached out to him on the fire escape. Using it as though it were an old friend who'd been waiting there for him all this time, he climbed down it to the street.

"Let them solve the problem of each other, themselves," he spoke out, walking farther and farther away. "That is now *their* destiny, not mine. God help them! It's they who've got the plague, not me!"

He knew where *he* was going, and directly too. He was returning back down that long, long highway, to the fatal fork in it, to the town where he was born, where the wrong direction had been chosen or forced upon him; he was going from the discovered cul de sac (*examine the bruises and scars on his poor head, ladies and gentlemen, if you don't believe that he found that absolute, ungiving wall at the end; see for yourselves*), to the other road which conceivably could take him somewhere. He would return to the particular fragrant spawning street of his childhood and begin there to search for the person he had been.

Must get there fast as possible. Run.

RUN!

Printed in March 2023
by Rotomail Italia S.p.A., Vignate (MI) - Italy